Understanding Baking

Pies, Tarts, Cakes and More

Rasheeda Hasan

UNDERSTANDING BAKING

Authorunit

17130 Van Buren Blvd., Ste. 238,

Riverside, CA 92504

877-826-5888

www.authorunit.com

ISBN: 978-1-960075-16-1 (Paperback)

ISBN: 978-1-960075-17-8 (Ebook)

Printed in the United States of America

Contents

Section *Pages*

Dedication

I Dedicate this Book to My Grandchildren, Muhammad, Marium, Sania, Aleena, Imaan, Mohsin, Nabihah, and Zainab

Epilogue

"An important decision I made was to resist playing the Blame Game. The day I realized that I am in charge of how I will approach problems in my life, that things will turn out better or worse because of me and nobody else, that was the day I knew I would be a happier and healthier person. And that was the day I knew I could truly build a life that matters.

-Steve Goodier

Legacy

Wealth is inheritance, and legacy is the part of yourself you leave behind-your soul, spirit, sweat, heart, love, dedication, courage, and example- that is your legacy, not numbers in bank.

-unknown

Introduction to Baking

Because cooking is an art, a dash of this and pinch of that or eyeballing ingredients works well. But baking requires precision at every step of the way. One has to observe several important rules to be a successful baker. Conquering baking and becoming a good baker requires the knowledge of equipment, ingredients, and chemistry behind the process of baking and most of all learning the techniques. The best way to do this is not to hesitate to try the same recipes over and over again and be ready to toss and restart failed recipes. Important thing is to measure the ingredients, such as flour, butter, sugar, salt, and leavening accurately with the right tools.

Measuring cups are used to measure dry ingredients which are essential for accuracy. To measure, cups are filled by spooning the ingredient to the top and leveling off by sweeping the excess with a knife or a spatula. The use of liquid measuring cups and measuring spoons is just as imperative for precision and the required results.

Heavier and shiny baking sheets made of aluminum distribute heat well and are ideal for perfectly baked goods. Also, it is better to avoid dark metal trays which absorb more heat and brown the baked items faster. Lining baking sheets with parchment paper makes it easy to slide the cookies onto the cooling rack. When the cookies are cooling they should be turned over to complete the cooling process and to prevent them from getting soggy.

Bake only one sheet of cookies on the middle rack in the center of the oven. For more than one batch of cookies, always allow sheets to cool completely before next use. Transfer the finished batch to a wire rack for cooling. The wire rack is the best tool because it allows cooling from all sides by letting the heat escape properly. Use a rack with closely spaced wires to provide support for cookies while cooling.

Here I have some baking tips and techniques for the home bakers to help develop skills and knowledge required for successful baking and bridge the gap between fear and fun.

When you know and understand how the baking process works, you can use foundation recipes on which countless variations can be built.

It is important to read the recipe carefully and use "mise en place" before starting the baking process. French use the term which means "everything in place". With this method, cooks get needed kitchen equipment and ingredients in place for ease of use. It is about having all your ingredients cleaned, diced, softened, melted, sifted, and measured before use. A bowl for garbage should also be on the counter as part of "mise en place" to save back and forth to the trash can.

Bring ingredients including eggs and butter to room temperature, when required.

Crack eggs on the counter rather than on the edge of a bowl and place them in separate bowls to prevent stray shell pieces in the batter.

Don't forget to grease cookie sheets, and cake pans thoroughly with a pastry brush.

Always keep in mind that ingredients quality plays a very important role in better results. Cutting costs is only natural but it is not worth the effort if the taste is compromised.

If ingredients such as baking powder, yeast, and spices are stored for a long time they lose their efficacy giving you baked products that are less than desirable. Therefore, you should replenish the old with the new supplies.

For cakes and cookies, it helps to sift flour more than once to incorporate air for a lighter texture.

When a recipe calls for nuts and berries, always toss them with flour before adding to the batter to prevent leaching the color or to prevent berries from settling down to the bottom.

Most recipe methods require beating butter and sugar to come to a creamy consistency before other ingredients are added. This creaming process helps to create bubbles resulting in fluffy and lighter baked goods. To maintain aeration of the batter, use folding motion to incorporate all the ingredients for the final batter. It is also important to let the batter rest for some time to let dry and wet ingredients fully combine.

In baking, it is necessary to use the correct equipment, and correct oven temperature for perfectly baked products.

Use timers to avoid the danger of overcooking and burning because of distractions. The use of a timer is very important in baking.

Ingredients in Baking

» Flour

Pie crust has four ingredients; flour, fat, salt, and ice water. When these ingredients work well with each other, the resulting crust is superb. Flour is a major ingredient and if you are not an experienced baker, you may think that all-purpose flour is the only flour to be used in baking. But there are different qualities and types of flours for different baked products. Different type of flour is well suited for different items; therefore, it is important to use the right type of flour for desired results.

All-purpose flour is most commonly used and is available either bleached or unbleached and is clearly labeled. Most people who make pies, scones, and other baked products, use bleached all-purpose flour. Unbleached all-purpose flour which is high in protein is commonly used for yeast bread.

Bread flour can be either bleached or unbleached and has more protein content than all-purpose. With 12% to 14% protein it is well suited for yeast bread. The bread products made with bread flour have better volume and texture because of their gluten strength. Bread made with bread flour is chewier with a brown crust.

Cake Flour has 8% to 10% protein and is used in cakes, muffins, cookies, and quick bread. It is a lot different from all-purpose because it is finely ground, with a silky smooth texture. Therefore, muffins and cakes made with it are fine-textured, tender, and delicious. Because it is chlorinated, it can absorb more liquid and sugar making the baked products moist and tender. Chlorination makes the cake flour a little acidic, which weakens gluten. Limiting the salt in the recipe also helps to tenderize, because salt strengthens gluten.

Self-rising flour can also be bleached or unbleached and has low protein with salt and leavening. It can also be made at home by adding baking powder and baking soda to all-purpose flour. It is best for tender biscuits, muffins, pancakes, and even some cakes. It should be stored tightly wrapped and used within six months to be effective. If it is old the leavening would lose its strength.

Whole wheat flour is made with whole grain as opposed to white flour which contains only the endosperm. Since whole wheat flour has the germ and bran added back to it, it is heavier and denser. For most Indian bread such as paratha, and chapattis whole wheat flour is a go-to flour.

Gluten-Free Flours are easily available. A great deal more information about gluten-free flours can be found at, kingarthurflour.com website. The site provides a wealth of information on everything baking.

» Sugar

Sugar is essential for baking. Apart from making baked goods sweet and tasty, it feeds the yeast and gives bread and other products shape and texture along with the taste. In baking, sugar is synonymous with granulated white sugar. It is used all over the world from sweetening a cup of tea to sweetening an entire slew of baked goods. But if you bake a lot, then you will be using different types of sugar. Following are some of the sugars which are used in baking, and each one has a different use.

1. White granulated sugar
2. Confectioners' sugar, icing or powdered sugar
3. Demerara sugar or Turbinado sugar
4. Superfine sugar or Castor sugar
5. Brown sugar (light and dark)
6. Muscovado or Barbados Sugar:

Granulated white sugar is synonymous with sweetening. It is the sugar everyone uses for sweetening beverages and desserts. A small amount of sugar is normally added to pastry doughs to create tenderness and enhance flavor. Also, cookies made with granulated white sugar will stay crispy for long. On the other hand, brown sugar cookies will go soft because it draws water in from the air over time. If a moist texture is desired in products like banana bread, brown sugar should be used. But for light and dry items granulated white sugar works perfectly. In her book Bakewise, Shirley Corriher notes that the use of white sugar in higher proportion "makes a very crisp cookie that stays crisp."

Confectioner's sugar is also called icing or powdered sugar. It is simply ground granulated white sugar mixed with cornstarch to prevent caking and used for frosting, and glazes.

Demerara and Turbinado are two varieties of raw sugars which cannot be used in place of white sugar. These sugars have large crystals and don't melt as easily and can be used to crust cakes and also for beverages.

Superfine or Castor Sugar has the smallest crystal, therefore is used in delicate desserts such as mousse, and meringues, etc. Its small crystals dissolve quickly in cold water and are widely used for beverages.

Brown sugar is of two kinds; light brown and dark brown sugar. The color difference reflects the percentage of molasses present in each. These sugars can be used interchangeably with white sugar. It only slightly changes the color and taste of the end product. In his book, The Sweet Spot, Pichet Ong, notes that brown sugar makes baked goods moister than white sugar because of the molasses content. In such cases, some adjustments may be necessary like decreasing the wet ingredients or adding the dry ones.

Muscovado sugar, also named Barbados sugar, is dark, and sticky brown. It is unrefined sugar from which molasses is not removed. It is mostly used in gingerbread, ginger cookies, and ice cream. It is also used in some savory dishes and barbecue sauces.

Sugar plays a very important part in baking. Understanding its role will help make you a better baker. Accuracy of the amount used is so important that many disasters in baking can be traced to mistakes in the amount of sugar used or its substitution. Sugar plays an important role in stabilizing meringues and creates tender baked goods such as muffins and cakes which do not dry out quickly.

Also, many delicious crunchy golden desserts owe their appeal to sugar. Heated sugar goes through a tremendous amount of chemical reactions and changes several shades of brown until it turns to caramel giving desserts their taste and color. And when sprinkled on top of pies and other goods it creates a crunchy delicious crystalized topping.

» Bakers Tips

Sugar syrup and caramel stages:

There are seven stages in caramel making.

1. Thread stage
2. Softball stage
3. Firm ball stage
4. Hardball stage
5. Soft crack stage
6. Hard crack stage
7. Caramel stage

The thread stage needs the temperature to reach up to 215°- 219°F. when you drop the syrup in ice water it forms loose threads.

The softball stage is when the temperature of the syrup registers 234°F-245°F.when the sugar syrup is dropped in ice water, it will form a soft, flexible ball. You can use this stage to make an extra soft topping for your desserts. It is used to make praline and fondant.

The firm ball stage registers 242°F - 248°F. at this stage syrup dropped in ice water will make a firm ball that won't flatten but can be manipulated to a required shape.

The hardball stage is attained when the temperature registers 250°F 266°F and when dropped in ice water makes a hardball that cannot be flattened.

Soft crack is at 270°F-290°F and forms flexible strands of candy that can still be bent.

Hard crack is at 300°F-310°F and forms strands that are brittle and break when bent.

Dark Caramel is at 345°F-350°F is a medium brown color and is used in flans, upside-down pineapple cake, and much more.

» Other Sweeteners

Maple syrup is derived from the sap of maple trees. It takes 40 gallons of sap for each gallon of syrup which makes it very expensive. Since it isn't used too much, it always goes a long way. It comes in grades which can be identified by color. The darkest color maple syrup is strongest.

Local grocery stores carry a version that lacks the flavor and taste of pure maple syrup and is less expensive because it is a combination of corn syrup, artificial flavorings, and a small amount of pure maple syrup.

Maple sugar is made by boiling the sap down until all the water is evaporated and is a lot sweeter than granulated sugar. It can be used as a sugar replacement in fruit pies or crumb topping.

Molasses is produced during stages of sugar refining. It is found as light, dark, or blackstrap molasses. It is used as a sweetener in food products, especially in baked goods to give them color, moistness, and flavor. Molasses also offers health benefits and has lots of medicinal uses.

Honey is comparable to granulated sugar in its sweetening power. Honey can be used to replace sugar in equal amounts. It tends to crystalize and can be liquefied either by placing it in hot water or microwave. When a microwave is used to bring honey to room temperature, care should be taken to prevent overheating. If it is overheated, its taste will be compromised.

Corn Syrup is liquid corn starch and is available in either light or dark form. Light corn syrup is sweet and flavorless, whereas dark corn syrup is flavored with caramel. The dark syrup is used in pies, such as pecan pie to give it flavor and color.

» Fats

Butter is one of the key ingredients in baking. It adds flavor and richness to food, but it can also be a leavening agent. For example, when the creaming method is used to make cake batters, butter and sugar are beaten together to create air bubbles. At this stage, eggs are incorporated. Water from the eggs and the fat create emulsion giving the batter stability. Butter also allows the steam and carbon dioxide to be trapped in the batter which causes cakes to rise while it bakes.

The same is true of Puff pastry. To make puff pastry, butter is rubbed into the flour to coat all the flour particles with butter. This inhibits the absorption of water and eggs into the flour, which prevents the development of gluten. While baking, the butter melts and creates steam which results in the creation of air pockets. That is how butter in the dough helps form delicate, light, and flakey pastries.

Each pound of butter measures two cups. Since one pound usually comes in 4 sticks, each stick measures ½ cup, or 8 tablespoons, and each tablespoon is ½ ounce. Butter is available as salted or unsalted. Almost all the recipes will call for unsalted because of its fresher, and sweeter taste. Although salted and unsalted butter can be used interchangeably, when you use salted butter, reduce the amount of salt used in the recipe.

Crisco, all-vegetable shortening is great for baking and can be used instead of butter. It has an advantage over other solid fats because it contains millions of fine bubbles to help in leavening. Since it does not melt even at warm room temperatures, there is no danger of it losing aeration which ensures flakey layers in the crust. Crisco is 100% fat contains no water and half the saturated fat of butter. It is an ideal ingredient for great texture but fails on the flavor front when compared to butter.

Vegetable Oils are unsaturated fats made from vegetables and tend to stay in liquid form at room temperature, whereas, saturated fats stay solid. Sunflower, safflower, corn oils are polyunsaturated and are good for lowering LDL cholesterol, but they can also lower HDL levels if used a lot.

For better results, it is advisable to use monounsaturated oils such as canola oil, peanut oil, other nut oil, and olive oil because they reduce the levels of LDLs, without affecting the levels of HDLs.

» Health Information on Fats

In baking, different kinds of fats, such as butter, margarine, oil, and Crisco are used. For tender, moist, and flakey baked goods fats are an integral part of the process. But it is better to understand the proper use of fat not only for best-baked goods but also for how and what to use for continued good health. Susan Purdy in her book, "Have Your Cake and Eat It,Too" says, "According to the American Heart Association, the average American diet drives as much as 40 percent of its total calories from fat." But the highly recommended amount by the authorities is 25 percent, and no more than 30 percent for health reasons. Since diets high in saturated fats, and high cholesterol are dangerous for health, reducing saturated fats and cholesterol in food intake is important to reduce the risk of heart disease, and clogged arteries which lead to strokes, and high blood pressure.

Although the word cholesterol has made fast inroads into the general consciousness, not many people understand what it is. It is a type of lipid found in animal fat. Our bodies need cholesterol for certain important body functions, and the body makes enough of it for the creation of cell walls, and other bodily substances. If one limits the dietary cholesterol it should not have any ill effects, because if you don't eat food high in cholesterol levels, the body produces enough to carry on its needed amount by producing more of it.

Dietary fat goes through the digestive process until it breaks down enough to be absorbed into the bloodstream and carried to the liver to be transformed into lipoproteins. Lipoproteins are bundles of triglycerides, and cholesterol, combined with proteins. They travel through the circulatory system to deliver the fats to the body cells where they are used for different functions. If you have been watching blood pressure and cholesterol levels, you have to monitor triglyceride levels also. Triglyceride is a type of fat (lipid) in your blood that can increase the risk of heart disease. When you consume more carbohydrates than your body can use, your body converts unused calories to triglycerides which are stored and then released for energy when needed. Your triglyceride count goes high if you regularly eat more calories than you can burn.

There are three types of lipoproteins: very-low-density(VLDLs), Low-density (LDLs), and high-density lipoprotein (HDLs). The main purpose of VLDLs is to distribute the triglycerides produced by the liver. Whereas, LDLs carry cholesterol. Now we have to look at what are the different functions of these different lipoproteins. VLDLs are the lowest density, and their job is to run through the circulatory system to make delivery of their cargo to the cells for the production of bodily energy. As they continue to do the job, they get lighter and the name changes to Low-density lipoproteins (LDLs) and the delivery continues until the supply is met with demand. This means that if all the fat is delivered there is no problem. But when excess is left over, LDLs will accumulate in the blood vessels. This results in plaque buildup which leads to narrowing and eventually blocking of the arteries and subsequently hindering the smooth blood flow through the system contributing to heart disease and strokes.

A heart-healthy diet is necessary to prevent plaque buildup which impedes blood flow and clot forming. HDL are heavier because they have less fat and are good cholesterol. They clean the circulatory system. When LDLs dumps the plaque, HDL which are high-density and carry less fat, suck up the plaque and return it to the liver for reprocessing and elimination. Blood tests are done to determine the level of cholesterol, and triglycerides. The recommended level of total cholesterol is 200, HDL of over 35, LDL of under 130, and triglycerides of 100 for a reduced risk of strokes and heart disease. If your levels vary considerably, it is important to go on a low-fat, low-cholesterol diet. I hope this will be helpful knowledge for the healthy use of necessary fats in our daily cooking and baking.

» Eggs

Eggs are an integral part of any baked product. Eggs are very nutritious. They play a very important role as they provide leavening, structure, and color to baked goods. A good rise and texture in baked goods are achieved with a balance in eggs and flour quantities used. Therefore, egg size is very important in baking. The pastry chefs are particular about using grade A large eggs weighing 2 ounces. Susan Purdy in her book, "Have Your Cake and Eat it, Too", says that if an egg looks particularly small to select a larger one or even measure its volume. It is good to know that a small egg weighs 1 ½ ounce, a medium egg weighs 1 ¾ ounce

While egg yolks give richness and color to baked goods, egg whites give a rise when they are gently folded in soufflés and doughs. Lightly beaten whole eggs or egg yolk are brushed on the surface of pies and biscuits to give them a shine.

To use eggs in baking, they should be removed from the refrigerator 30 minutes before using. If there is not enough time to do that, place them in a bowl of warm water for a few minutes. Room temperature eggs not only blend and emulsify well with other ingredients but also gain more volume when beaten.

When the eggs are used in recipes where they are combined with hot liquid they are tempered to bring up the temperature of the eggs without scrambling them. If all the hot liquid is added all at once, the eggs would scramble. Raise the temperature of the eggs by slowly adding hot sauce or milk while stirring. When the temperature of the egg mixture is raised enough, it is poured back into the hot milk saucepan to finish cooking. This tempering technique is used when custards, puddings, and sauces are made.

» Chocolate

Chocolate is used in different forms depending on the recipe. Since there is a wide range of chocolate treats like brownies, cupcakes, truffles, icing, and ganache, each recipe requires certain important techniques to incorporate chocolate for successful completion. Knowledge of the type of chocolate to be used in a specific recipe is extremely important. The process of melting chocolate has to be learned and you have to keep certain guidelines in mind to avoid mishaps.

1. for melting chocolate evenly, make sure that all the pieces are of even size.
2. chocolate will seize at the hint of water; therefore, everything which comes in contact with chocolate has to be completely dry. The correct way is to melt over low heat and stir frequently. You can melt chocolate in a double boiler or microwave. When melting chocolate in a microwave oven, it is imperative to select a microwave-safe bowl, which does not get too hot, to prevent scorching. If using microwave, heat chocolate for 30 seconds, then remove from the microwave and stir. Continue the process until most, but not all, the chocolate is melted. Remove and stir until thoroughly smooth.

The traditional method of melting chocolate in a double boiler requires a saucepan with 1-inch water, and a heat-safe bowl on top of the saucepan so that the bottom of the bowl is not touching the water. Water is brought to a gentle simmer for steam to warm the bowl. Add chopped chocolate to the bowl and stir frequently until chocolate is smooth and evenly melted.

» Ganache

Classic ganache is made by blending chocolate and heavy cream. Ganache can be made with butter or cream. The one made with butter has a velvety glow to it, whereas the cream ganache has a glossy shine. Butter and cream are interchangeable in making ganache. Both butter and cream contain water, fat, and dairy product. With a difference that the quantity of the dairy product in cream is slightly more than it is in butter. And ganache is made in three different grades.

1. Medium ganache contains an equal amount of bittersweet or semisweet chocolate and heavy cream.
2. Soft ganache contains 2 parts of heavy cream to each part of chocolate.
3. Firm ganache contains two parts of chocolate to one part of heavy cream.

According to Shirley O. Corriher, it is always better to add chocolate to the hot liquid, rather than pouring hot liquid over the chocolate. The heat from the liquid will melt the chocolate. Once melted, whisking will result in a smooth, shiny ganache. The cold liquid should never be added to the melted chocolate as it can cause the chocolate to seize.

» Cocoa Powder

Cocoa powder is used in a lot of chocolate baked goods. It is always confusing when you see cocoa powder and Dutch-processed cocoa powder. Here I am going to try to demystify the difference between Dutch-process and natural cocoa powder. I think you need to know what is cocoa powder. It is a byproduct of cocoa beans. There are two types; natural cocoa powder and Dutch-processed cocoa powder. If during the processing, cocoa beans are washed in an alkaline solution of potassium bicarbonate to neutralize its acidity, it becomes unfit to react with baking soda which is also alkaline. This alkaline product is called Dutch-processed and is always paired with baking powder in recipes. This chemically different product is darker, mild, and dissolves in water.

On the other hand, natural cocoa powder is a product of cocoa beans that is acidic, strong, and has a concentrated taste of chocolate. because it is acidic it is used with baking soda in the recipe. Since baking soda is alkaline, acidity in the natural cocoa powder helps baked goods to rise. In most recipes, this difference is not explained and results in failed recipes. In baking aisles of supermarkets, the cocoa powder sold is usually natural. If the recipe simply says cocoa powder, use natural cocoa powder. But it is important to stick to the recipe for success. Otherwise, you can end up with flat cakes.

» Leavening agents and how they work

To most home cooks, leaveners mean baking powder and baking soda, and they are the primary chemical leaveners used in home cooking.

Baking soda (sodium bicarbonate) is alkaline and when combined with acid gives out carbon dioxide; therefore, works well with acidic ingredients, such as chocolate, sour cream, molasses, and buttermilk. Recipes with baking soda need acidic ingredients, and moisture to create bubbles for releasing carbon dioxide which causes the baked goods to rise. Since baking soda reactions begin immediately after mixing, baking should begin right away, or else the baked goods will fall flat. Baking soda is 3-4x stronger than baking powder. It is also important to have balance in the baking soda and acid to make tasty baked goods. Too much baking soda will give a metallic taste to baked goods.

Baking powder can be made by mixing 1 tablespoon baking soda, with 2 tablespoons cream of tartar, and 1½ tablespoons cornstarch (optional). Baking powder comes as single-acting or double-acting. Single-acting powders are activated as soon as they are mixed with moisture and should be baked immediately. Since double-acting powders react in two phases they can stand for a while before baking. Some gas is released when at room temperature, but most of the gas is released when in the hot oven. Shirley Corriher says, "In most recipes, 1 teaspoon (5g) baking powder or ¼ teaspoon (1g) baking soda leavens 1 cup of flour." When too much leavening is used the result is undesirable. Baking powder and baking soda do not make bubbles, but their gases enlarge bubbles created during the creaming or mixing process of cake making. So how are the bubbles created for the leaveners to work successfully and help rise baked goods? Mixing, normally considered as a way to blend ingredients and is a vital part of the process of leavening. Bakers depend on mixing methods to incorporate a lot of bubbles into the batter. How to create proper size bubbles is an important technique that requires a balanced amount of ingredients along with an understanding of the process. Chef Ronald Mesnier was referred to as saying that speed of mixing is of utmost importance. High-speed whipping creates large bubbles which, during the cooking, rise to the top and pop. But if you first beat fat alone, and then fat and sugar mixture long enough at a medium speed, a massive amount of air bubbles will be incorporated to give you a light, well-aerated cake with a good volume. You must remember that you have to keep the fat cool throughout the process by returning the bowl to the freezer for 5 minutes if it starts to feel warm. You should also limit the gluten formation by controlling the amount of stirring when all of the liquid and flour is already added. Bubbles are created during first creaming the fat and sugar, and then eggs are added but this does not change the volume. When the prepared batter is in the oven, steam from the liquid acts as a leavener and inflates the existing bubbles to make the cake light and airy.

The cream of tartar is powdered acid, which is formed during the fermentation of grapes into wine. It is used with baking soda. It reacts with baking soda and acts as a leavening agent during baking. It also stabilizes egg whites, and it helps to prevent the sugar from crystallizing.

A good substitute for baking soda and cream of tartar is baking powder. Other substitutes for the cream of tartar are lemon juice and vinegar. But since these are liquids taking the place of powder, the level of liquid has to be adjusted in the recipe. And you have to be aware that it can also change the flavor and texture of the end product.

Gelatin is a product of collagen, protein from bones, and connective tissue. It is unflavored and is available in the granulated form in small envelopes, and sometimes in sheets that have to be reconstituted by soaking in water. If you buy it in envelopes it contains 2 teaspoons (¼ ounces) 7 grams. Each cup of liquid would require at least 1 teaspoon of granulated gelatin.

Liquids include water, milk, cream, sour cream, yogurt, fruit juices, alcohol, honey, molasses, oil, melted butter, eggs, and coffee. Liquids play a variety of very important roles in the baking process. They dissolve not only salt and sugar, but also create steam to push apart the cells created during the batter-making process and aerate the batter or the dough. It is the presence of liquid that initiates the binding of proteins to create a network of gluten which gives the baking products their structure. And also moistens the leavening agent to release the CO2 which is needed for the rising of the baked goods.

Gluten formation is activated when water is added to the flour and is of critical importance in the baking of bread. Whereas in making pie crust a special technique is used to avoid gluten formation to keep the product tender and crumbly. For tenderness, flour proteins are well greased to prevent them from joining water or each other to form tough gluten. That is done by rubbing fat into the flour and keeping the use of water at a minimum to minimize gluten production.

Liquids such as sour cream, buttermilk, and juices are acidic and inhibit the production of gluten, they are very favorable ingredients for tender pie and tart crust

» Dairy Products

Milk and milk products are used in baking for moisture, color, and tenderness. Milk products contain fat and cholesterol along with a variety of vitamins, and mineral. Low-fat milk is obtained by removing fat and cholesterol but has extra calcium in it.

Milk, buttermilk, or sour cream are three ingredients, and in general, the liquid ingredients portion of a cake is overlooked and yet plays a very important role in the baking process. The use of dairy products and their substitution requires an understanding of the properties of these items and how they affect the recipes in which they are used. Since these three products contain varying amounts of acidity and fat, cakes made with milk, buttermilk, or sour cream will have a difference in the coarseness of the crumb and flavor of the cake.

Milk, buttermilk, and sour cream provide a different level of fat and acidity which changes the texture and color of the cake. Milk provides 9 grams of fat per cup with lower acidity. This lack of acidity results in the coarse crumb. Buttermilk is low fat with a slightly higher acidity than milk resulting in a cake that is tenderer and more flavorful. Sour cream provides similar acidity to buttermilk but with 40 grams of fat per cup. Since acidity increases the coarseness and fat is a great tenderizer that carries flavors, it creates a balance. This balance in acidity and fat level has a great impact on the outcome. Cakes made with sour cream are very tender and flavorful.

» Kitchen Equipment

The following tools are necessary and usually, most kitchens have them.

Dry measuring cups are used for measuring dry ingredients and also semi-solid ingredients such as jam, and sour cream. Normally scoop and sweep method is used in which ingredients such as flour are scooped up with a cup and the excess is swept with a knife or spatula to level it off. But for a better result, measuring cups should be filled by spooning the ingredient to the top and leveled off by sweeping the excess off with a knife or a spatula.

Liquid measuring cups usually are heat-resistant glass with a spout. For measuring pour in the ingredient and set it on a level surface to read the measurement at eye level.

Measuring spoons come in a set ranging from ¼ teaspoon to 1 tablespoon. These are good for measuring salt, pepper, and other spices. It is always better not to measure directly over the bowl to prevent an extra amount from going in. While measuring liquid such as vanilla, fill it to the rim.

Sieves have several important uses in baking. It is used to combine flour, yeast, and salt into a bowl. It also aerates the flour and makes cakes and cookies tender and light in texture.

Microplane is a great tool for zesting limes and lemons. I also use it to grate frozen ginger root, nutmeg, and parmesan cheese when needed.

Mandolin is an extremely versatile tool. It comes with 3 or 4 slicing blades. Even if you use one or two blades for basic slicing needs, you will find that it cuts the prep time significantly, and is fun to use.

Offset Spatula is used for smoothing icing on cakes, as well as to smooth layers of sauces in casseroles and lasagñas.

Whisk is used to incorporate dry and liquid ingredients. Sometimes more than one whisk is used to get a better result in getting volume in whipped cream, and egg white to make the meringue.

Pastry Blenders are great to cut butter into the flour in pastry making process.

Spatulas are used for cleaning the sides of the bowls while cake batter is being made. It is also used for the top layer of cheese in lasagña and many other dishes where leveling of ingredients is required.

Kitchen Shears can be used to cut excess dough from the edges of the pastry when making pies. They not only facilitate the cutting but are easy to maneuver than a knife in removing chicken bones etc.

Kitchen Scales should be a part of every serious kitchen. When I have something which is beyond the capacity of the scale, I weigh in batches. But there are digital scales available and are very easy to use.

Cooling Racks are invaluable equipment in the kitchen. They come in all shapes and sizes, footed and made of metal wire or mesh. Since they are about ½ inch high, the air can circulate freely around the baked goods to cool them evenly on all sides.

Thermometers are used for baking, and candy making. An oven thermometer is recommended for adjusting the inaccuracy of oven heat.

Pastry Scraper is versatile. It is used not only in making dough and pastry crust but also for leveling the ingredients in measuring cups, transferring cut-up fruit and vegetables to different containers, and much more. They come with a stainless steel blade and handle and work perfectly. They also come with plastic handles and wooden handles.

Strainers come in different sizes and mesh densities. It is always a good idea to keep an assortment for different uses. You can use them to aerate the flour and sugar mixture and to remove lumps from the custard fillings.

Glass pie plates are highly recommended for they are not only inexpensive but they brown the bottom crust extremely well. It is also easy to see the progress of the pie when still cooking. Cutting in the plate itself is easy and it does not leave scratch marks. The best part is that they are extremely easy to clean.

For experienced bakers or bakeries, different pie baking utensils are available.

Baking Sheets and cookie sheets are the names for shallow rimmed or rimless rectangular pans used for baking cookies and pastries. Rimless sheets are useful when you want to slide the already baked cookies onto a rack to cool. But the rimmed baking sheets which are also called half-sheet pans are extremely useful in the kitchen. They are used for baking sheet cakes, vegetables, nuts, or any number of things.

Electric Blender is an essential utensil in a modern-day kitchen. In the blink of an eye, it purees, grates, chops, minces, and blends liquids and solids.

The Food Processor makes the cooking a breeze removing all the cumbersome and time-consuming chores. It chops, cuts, mixes, and blends ingredients in required amounts for instant use.

Electric Stand Mixer is a must for making bread dough, creaming butter, and sugar for cakes. These tedious cooking tasks become effortless when you have an appliance such as this.

Immersion Blender reduces not only the tasks involved in cooking but also the cleaning time is also reduced several folds. It can blend all sorts of beans, vegetables, and prepare sauces in the vessels they are cooked in without the hassles of transferring from the pot to the blender and vice versa. It can be washed and stored in a jiffy which makes it one of my favorite tools in the kitchen.

» All About Pastry Crust

Pastry making is synonymous with baking. There are zillion desserts that use pastry crust in one form or another. My first encounter with pastry making or eating was in 1966 when I was in England and got a chance to eat pies, pastries, tarts, and a slew of other baked goods. Sweet and savory pies, pasties, and tarts became a special part of my diet.

I had some really good friends in England who took on themselves to teach me how to make homemade pies. Margaret Dobson had a large part in exposing me to English food. I learned a lot from her and other friends. I have been making and learning more and more about different techniques to get better at it. Because of my love for baking, I decided that I also wanted to share my experiences and knowledge of this craft with those who have the desire to eat pies and tarts and learn how to make them at home.

It may be a breeze to make wonderfully flaky, tender, beautifully golden brown pies for an experienced baker, but a starting baker needs time to develop the skill to understand exact proportions of flour, fat, and water to be successful. Another more important factor is learning the techniques of combining ingredients to make a good crust.

The techniques used in flakey pastry crust aim at minimizing gluten production by using very little water with minimum kneading and allowing the dough to rest. This is done by coating the flour with fat before adding any water. During baking, steam rises and pushes the layers of dough to create crumbly and flakey pastry.

American bakers exclusively use water to make the crust, but Italian bakers use eggs in place of water. I always wondered how some of these pastry crust recipes with egg as an ingredient did not have any water until I found out that egg is 75% water and provides the needed liquid ingredient. To make a pie crust, add the butter or shortening to the flour and use a pastry blender, mixer, or your hands to work the fat into the flour until it resembles breadcrumbs with some pea-sized pieces of butter remaining. Having some of the butter in larger pieces creates flakiness in the baked crust. At this stage, either add an egg or start adding water in tablespoons until the dough is moist enough and clumps together when pressed in your hand. Transfer the dough onto a plastic wrap and bring all the loose flour to form a disc with a smooth surface and edges. If it is enough for a double crust, divide it into two portions. The larger portion should be for the bottom crust and the smaller for the top. Wrap each one in plastic wrap and refrigerate for 30 minutes or overnight.

When the dough is chilled, remove it from the refrigerator and set it on the countertop to temper (soften) it for ease in rolling. This tempering process could take anywhere from 5 to 20 minutes depending on how long it was chilled.

» Pastry Rolling Techniques

To roll, place the dough on a well-floured surface and roll pressing from the center to the edge toward the noon position but easing the pressure near the edge to prevent it from becoming too thin. Keep turning the pastry 45 degrees and continue to roll from center to the edge making sure that it does not stick to the counter. Lift from one side and sprinkle some flour under to prevent sticking while being careful not to over flour. Continue to roll until it is 12 to 14 inches in diameter and 1/8 inch in thickness.

Once the pie crust is rolled and ready, transfer it to the pie pan without it falling apart. To line the pie pan perfectly, you can use different techniques. One way is to roll the crust on a rolling pin and gently unroll it into the pie pan away from you. Another method is to fold it in a half or a quarter and transfer it into the pie pan by keeping the point in the center of the pie pan, and then unfold to line it. Gently lift the edges of the dough to ease it into the bottom and sides of the pie pan. Trim the overhang. Dock the bottom and sides of the crust, but not all the way through, and refrigerate to keep it cool to prevent it from shrinking while it cooks.

» Blind-Baking Basics

In blind baking empty piecrust is baked partly or completely to firm it up and prevent it from getting soggy. In pies or tart where the filling needs cooking, the crust is blind-baked only partly so it won't overcook. But in recipes where filling does not need any further cooking or needs cooking for a short time, the crust is cooked until it is golden brown.

When the pie pan is lined with crust it is important to chill it before baking. Because the process of rolling, and lining the plate can cause the butter to soften which could result in the crust caving in when the heat of the oven hits it. Therefore, chilling the crust before baking helps to maintain its integrity.

Once chilled, line the crust with parchment paper. To fit the paper well, crumple the paper and then straighten it to line the crust. Fill the lined plate well with some weights like beans, rice, or whatever dry grains you have on hand.

Preheat the oven to 425°F and place the rack in the center of the oven. Place the prepared pie pan with weights to bake for 7 to 10 minutes. Remove from the oven and let it cool slightly before removing the beans and paper lining. Let the oven heat up and return the crust to the oven for another 10 minutes to get it golden brown when required. When ready, transfer to a rack and let it cool completely while you prepare the filling.

Pies, and Tarts

» Short Crust Pastry Recipes

In this section, I am going to include all my kitchen-tested recipes for home cooks to create pies and tarts with their favorite fillings. These recipes for pie crusts and toppings work for traditional pies and tarts. Before we begin, I think you need to understand that the pie shell is the crust to cover the bottom, and it could be pie crust or crumb crust. The pie topping or top crust fully covers the top of the filling. Once these basic terminologies and techniques are mastered, you can use variation in any recipe. I have several different recipes for making pie crust on the following pages, and also have suggestions for their possible use. But you should try your twists, experiment, and have fun.

Double-Crust Pie pastry

A lot of people are scared to even attempt to make pie crust. But it is not difficult. Anyone can do it. It takes less time to make it than to go to the store to buy it. Once you know how to make the pastry crust, you are equipped to create an immensely gratifying variety of pastry-based desserts.

2½ cups all-purpose flour
¼ teaspoon salt
2 tablespoon sugar
10 tablespoons (1¼ stick) unsalted, cold butter, cut into small dice
1/3 cup Crisco
6 tablespoons ice-cold water or just enough to make the dough

- Cut up the butter and return to the refrigerator until ready to use.
- In a food processor bowl, process flour, salt, and sugar until well incorporated. Add butter and Crisco and pulse until it resembles coarse crumbs with some pea-sized pieces remaining. Add water a little at a time until it forms a moist dough.
- Remove to a working surface and knead lightly until smooth. Then divide the dough into two balls, one just slightly smaller than the other. Flatten each one into a disc and wrap into a plastic sheet, and refrigerate for, at least, 1 hour or overnight.
- When ready to use, roll the larger disc to make a shell to fit the 9-inch pie plate.
- A smaller disc is rolled out to top the pie filling.

Single-Crust Pie pastry

1¼ cups all-purpose flour

¼ teaspoon salt

1/3 cup butter-flavored shortening, although regular Crisco also works well.

4 to 5 tablespoons ice water

- In a food processor bowl, pulse flour and salt to combine. Add Crisco and pulse until it resembles coarse crumbs with some pea-sized pieces remaining. Add water a little at a time until it forms a moist dough.
- Remove to a working surface and knead lightly until smooth. Make a ball and then flatten it into a disc and wrap it into a plastic sheet. Refrigerate for 1 hour or overnight.
- When ready to use, roll on a well-floured surface into a circle. Rolling action should always be from the center to the edge. Flour the board whenever necessary to prevent dough from sticking to the surface. Repair any tears by bringing the dough together with wet fingers. Fold the dough in half and place it on the pie plate then unfold to fit in the bottom and sides covering the edges of the plate to ease the crimping.

Cream Cheese Pie Dough

This recipe calls for vinegar. Vinegar prevents the formation of gluten making the crust tender and flaky.

1½ cup all-purpose flour
½ teaspoon salt
½ cup (^ tablespoons) cold unsalted butter, cut into small pieces
4 oz. cream cheese, cut into small pieces
1 egg yolk
1 teaspoon cider vinegar
2 teaspoons cold water

- Sieve flour, and salt in a large bowl. Add cold butter and cream cheese and rub with the tips of your fingers until the mixture resembles crumbs.
- Beat egg yolk lightly, add water and vinegar and add to the flour in small portions and mix until the dough comes together in a ball. Flatten the dough ball into a disc and wrap it in a plastic sheet and refrigerate for 30 minutes or even overnight. When ready to roll, remove the dough from the fridge and let it soften enough to make it easy to roll.
- Roll on a well-floured surface into a circle. Rolling action should always be from the center to the edge. Flour the board whenever necessary to prevent dough from sticking to the surface. Repair any tears by bringing the dough together with wet fingers. Fold the dough in half and place it on the pie plate then unfold to fit.
- Ease the dough in the pie plate to properly fit in the bottom and sides of the pie pan with some overhang to ease crimping.
- Remove the excess dough either with knife or kitchen scissor. You can use this dough to make cookies.

Paté Brisée

Paté Brisée is a French version of the dough with basic ingredients which are flour, salt, butter, and cold water. It is useful for both sweet and savory pies.

8 ounces (1 cup) all-purpose flour
1 teaspoon sugar
Heavy pinch salt
4 ounces (1 stick) cold, unsalted butter, cut into pieces
2 tablespoons or needed amount ice water

- Sift flour, salt, and sugar in a bowl to combine and aerate.
- Add softened butter and rub with tips of the finger until the mixture resembles crumbs, or until dough holds together when squeezed.
- Add ice water one tablespoon at a time and gather all the flour and more water with a spritzer bottle to control the amount, if needed, until the dough can be made into a ball. Wrap the ball in a plastic wrap to chill for 30 minutes or more.
- When ready to roll, remove the dough from the fridge and let it soften enough to make it easy to roll.
- Roll pastry to fit a 9-inch pie pan with a removable bottom. Transfer dough to the pie pan. If the pastry overhangs, roll the rolling pin on the pan, which will cut all the extra pastry and giving the pastry tart a shape. Dock the bottom with a fork to prevent bubbles from forming during the cooking process. Freeze until firm, for about 15 minutes, because warm pastry can collapse when put into the hot oven. Line the pastry with parchment paper, and fill it with pie weights or beans for blind baking.
- Bake in a 400-degree oven for 15 minutes or until light brown.

Remove from the oven and then remove pie weights and parchment paper. Return the pastry to the oven for another 5 to 10 minutes covering the edges with aluminum foil or pastry guard to prevent the edges from burning. Remove and let it cool before filling.

Paté Sablée (Sugar Cookie Dough)

Paté sablée has a cookie-like dough that crumbles with the pressure of your fork. Although its name translates to" sandy", but it makes a dough ideal for any tart.

½ cup (1 stick) 8 tablespoons unsalted butter, room temperature
1/3 cup powdered (powdered) sugar
1 large egg yolk
1¼ cup all-purpose flour
½ teaspoon salt
1 tablespoon cream or milk

- Cream butter and sugar in a standing electric mixer until it is pale and fluffy. Beat in the egg yolk until fully combined scraping the bottom and sides by stopping a few times.
- Add flour and salt, and beat until well combined but not overbeaten. The dough is ready when it holds when you squeeze in your hand. If not, add 1 tablespoon milk or cream.
- Transfer to a plastic wrap and bring in all the loose flour to form a dough ball.
- Flatten it to a disc and refrigerate for at least 1 hour or up to 2 days.
- When ready to roll, remove the dough from the fridge and let it soften enough to make it easy to roll.
- Roll it between two sheets of plastic wrap to prevent sticking to the work surface. Roll from center to the edges making sure not to press on the edges.
- Roll it up to 2 inches larger than the pan. Remove the top layer of the plastic sheet and invert the crust into the tart pan. Peel away the plastic wrap and gently press the crust into the bottom and sides of the pan. Trim the edges and loosely wrap the crust in plastic to refrigerate for 30 minutes.
- Once chilled, line the crust with parchment paper. To fit the

paper well, crumple the paper and then straighten it to line the crust. Fill the lined plate well with some weights like beans, rice, or whatever dry grains you may have on hand.

- Preheat the oven to 425° F. and place the rack in the center of the oven, and bake for 7 to 10 minutes. Remove from the oven and let it cool slightly before removing the beans and paper lining. Let the oven heat up again and return the crust to the oven for another 10 minutes to get it golden brown when required. For the last 10 minutes, cover the edges with a piece of foil, or a pie guard to prevent edges from burning. When ready, transfer to a rack and let it cool completely while you prepare the filling.

Paté Sucre (Classic Tart Dough)

It is a sweet pastry that is sturdy and good for making tarts. Since it contains sugar and egg yolks, its texture is suitable for it to be unmolded while it is easy to break clean under a fork. Essentially it is a crust that is tender and crumbly and sublimely delicious.

2 cup all-purpose flour
2 tablespoon powdered sugar
¼ teaspoon salt
1 cup (2 sticks) cold unsalted butter, cut into small dice
1 large egg lightly beaten
½ teaspoon vanilla extract
Ice water, needed for the dough to come together

- Pulse flour, powdered sugar, and salt in a food processor to combine. Add butter and pulse until the mixture resembles coarse crumbs.
- Lightly beat eggs, and vanilla extract to combine and sprinkle on the surface evenly over the dry ingredients and pulse until the dough comes together. If the dough is still dry, add some water and pulse more.
- Divide the dough in half and make two dough balls. Pat each one into a disc, wrap in plastic, and refrigerate for 30 minutes or overnight before using.
- When ready to roll, remove the dough from the fridge and let it soften enough to roll.
- Roll it between two sheets of plastic wrap to prevent it from sticking to the work surface. Roll from center to the edges making sure not to press on the edges.
- Roll it up to 2 inches larger than the pan. Remove the top layer of the plastic sheet and invert the crust into the tart

pan. Peel away the plastic wrap and gently press the crust into the bottom and sides of the pan. Trim the edges and loosely wrap the pastry-lined tart pan in plastic to refrigerate for 30 minutes.

- Once chilled, line the crust with parchment paper. To fit the paper well, crumple the paper and then straighten it to line the crust. Fill the pan well with some weights like beans, rice, or whatever dry grains you may have on hand.
- Preheat the oven to 425° F. and place the rack in the center of the oven. Place the prepared tart pan with weights to bake in the oven and bake for 7 to 10 minutes. Remove from the oven and let it cool slightly before removing the beans and paper lining. Let the oven heat up again and return the crust to the oven for another 10 minutes to get it golden brown. For the last 10 minutes, cover the edges with foil or pie guard to prevent edges from burning. When ready, transfer to a rack and let it cool completely while you prepare the filling.

Hot Water Pastry for Meat Pies

Hot water crust is used to make savory pies, and especially for pork pies. Also traditionally used for making hand pies.

8 ounces of bread flour, plus some for dusting
Pinch salt
½ cup water
1 tablespoon milk
1 stick unsalted butter
To Glaze:
1 large egg yolk

- Sift the flour and salt into a bowl and set aside.
- In a small saucepan, put water, milk, and butter and start heating on a low heat until the fat melts completely.
- Turn the heat up and bring the liquid to a boil. When it comes to a boil, pour it onto the flour and mix using a spoon until it comes together in a dough. Turn the dough out onto a work surface and knead very lightly for a short time.
- Since the dough is used while still warm to make pies, take 2/3 of the dough and divide it into 6 equal parts. Roll each one into a ball and place one in each of the molds in a large muffin tin. Using your thumb press the pastry into the bottom, then up along the edges bringing a ¼ inch lip over the rim.
- Fill it with the prepared filling.
- Roll out the remaining 1/3 of the pastry fairly thin, and cut six 3 ¼ inches round to make lids for the pies.
- Using a pastry brush, paint with a little egg yolk around the edges of each. Press a lid on each pie with the egg side down.
- Using a fork press on the edges to seal the pastry along the edges.

- Glaze the top with the remaining egg yolk and cut a hole for steam. Put in the preheated 350° F. oven and, bake for 30 to 40 minutes.
- Once they are ready, remove them from the tin and place them on the baking sheet to make the sides and base crispy.

Choux Pastry (Pate a Choux)

Choux pastry is versatile. French use it for a variety of pastry items. In Spain and Latin America, it is used to make churros. French beignets are simply referred to as fritters are made with pate a choux pastry.

1 stick butter, cubed
1 cup water
1 teaspoon sugar or
Pinch salt
1 cup all-purpose flour, sifted
4 eggs

- In a saucepan, mix water, butter, sugar, or salt, for the desired taste, and bring it to a boil.
- Add sifted flour to the hot mixture after removing it from the heat.
- Return the saucepan to heat and vigorously stir the contents until the mixture becomes a firm dough and leaves the sides of the saucepan. Overcooking will make the dough oily.
- Remove the saucepan from heat and let it cool sufficiently to prevent eggs from curdling when eggs are added one at a time.
- Beating each egg thoroughly before adding another one is important to remove any trace of either white or yolk in the mixture.
- Once the dough comes to a good consistency, allow it to cool before using.
- It can stay for 2 to 3 hours without any problem.

Crumb Crust Recipes

Graham Cracker Crust

Crumb crust is used for tart shells. This crust is extremely easy to make and used for cheesecakes and cream pies, such as Banana Cream pie, custard pies with Meringue topping.

20 squares Graham crackers (10 sheets)
¼ cup sugar
5 tablespoons unsalted butter, melted
pinch salt
1 teaspoon light corn syrup
Nonstick cooking spray

- Preheat the oven to 350° F.
- In a food processor bowl, process crackers to fine crumbs.
- Add sugar and give a few pulses. Sugar is important because sugar crystals help bind the crumbs together.
- Add melted butter to the processor in a thin stream while the processor is running. Add salt during the process.
- Add syrup to the processor while it is running until well combined.
- Lightly grease a 9-inch springform pan with cooking spray. Transfer the processed crumbs to the pan and press in the bottom and 1½ inch up the sides of the pan firmly and evenly by using a measuring cup.
- Refrigerate for 15 minutes. And then bake for 15 minutes, or until golden brown.
- Cool the shell completely before adding your desired filling.

Chocolate Graham Cracker Crust

20 squares graham crackers (10 sheets), broken into pieces
¼ cup sugar
½ teaspoon ground cinnamon
pinch salt
5 tablespoons unsalted butter, melted
1 teaspoon light corn syrup
Non-stick cooking spray

- Preheat the oven to 350°F.
- In a bowl of a food processor, process the graham crackers, sugar, cinnamon, salt, butter, and corn syrup until it is fine crumbs.
- Spray a springform pan with non-stick cooking spray and transfer the crumbs into it. With a measuring cup press the crumbs in the bottom of the pan while bringing the crust 1-inch up the sides.
- Refrigerate for 15 minutes. Then bake for 15 minutes, or until golden brown.
- Cool the shell for 30 minutes before adding your desired filling.
- The prepared crust can be stored for up to 1 day, covered with foil, at room temperature.

Chocolate-Nut Crust

This crust is adapted from Shirley Corriher's Bakewise: The Hows and Whys of Successful Baking.

¾ cup chopped walnuts
½ cup (8 tablespoons) unsalted, cold butter, cut in small dice (divided) use
¼ cup brown sugar, packed
1 cup all-purpose flour, spooned into a measuring cup and then leveled
½ teaspoon salt
1 oz. unsweetened baking chocolate, grated
1 teaspoon vanilla extract
1 tablespoon water
Non-stick cooking spray

- Preheat the oven to 375°F with the rack in the center of the oven.
- Spread walnut on a baking tray and roast in a preheated oven for 5 to 7 minutes. Remove from the oven and toss them with 2 tablespoons butter and set aside to cool.
- Put brown sugar, flour, salt, and roasted walnuts in a food processor bowl and process until the nuts are really fine. Add the remaining 6 tablespoons butter and pulse on and off to incorporate the butter into the mixture. Transfer the mixture into a large bowl.
- Using a Microplane or a fine grater, grate chocolate into the flour mixture and stir to mix.
- Mix vanilla and water in a cup, and sprinkle on the flour mixture in small portions and toss until it is crumbly.
- Spray a springform pan with non-stick cooking spray and transfer the crumbs into it. With a measuring cup press the crumbs in the bottom of the pan while bringing the crust

1-inch up the sides. Refrigerate for 15 minutes. Then bake for 15 minutes, or until golden brown. Let it cool completely before filling.

Crumble Toppings

Crumb toppings are a great way of offering change by using crumb on top while keeping traditional pastry crust on the bottom. It adds extra sweetness and texture to the soft fruit fillings. You can make crumb topping ahead of time and refrigerate for up to a week.

Sugar Crumb topping:

½ cup unbleached all-purpose flour
1/3 cup firmly packed dark brown sugar
1 teaspoon cinnamon
½ teaspoon ground nutmeg
¼ teaspoon salt
5 tablespoons unsalted, cold butter, cut in cubes

- Thoroughly mix flour, sugar, cinnamon, nutmeg, and salt in a large bowl.
- Add butter and use a pastry blender or tips of your fingers to incorporate the butter into the flour until it forms pea-size pieces.
- Once the filling is poured into the shell, sprinkle the prepared topping evenly all over the filling making sure to cover it completely. Bake according to the recipe directions.

*For a variety of different tastes, you can add chopped nuts, such as walnuts, almonds, and pecans, or whatever you wish.

Dessert Pies, Tarts and Cakes

Apple pie is so popular that it is not only consumed regularly in most homes but also at a lot of parties as dinner-dessert. One out of every five Americans prefers apple pie for dessert.

Apple Pies come in a variety of crusts and topping. There are double-crust, single crusts, apple galettes, apple tartlets, apple crumble with a pie shell and crumb topping, and much more.

Here are different homemade crust recipes to choose from for home bakers. It offers a chance to pick any one recipe at a given time and practice the art of pie baking. There are, of course, ready-made pie crusts available in grocery stores for those home bakers with a time constraint.

Canned fillings are also available in the grocery stores which considerably cut the dessert making time, and are easy to use. All it needs is the addition of some required mixings to the canned filling before pouring it into the pie shell. Pies made with fresh fruit fillings are delicious and can be a bit of a challenge as they require preparation time. Fruits have to be peeled, deseeded, and cut into equal size pieces for even cooking. Fruits such as apples need to be either soaked in acidulated water or tossed in lemon juice to prevent browning. Some say that when soaked, apples absorb a lot of water which is released during cooking resulting in a soft and mushy filling. To prevent that apples should be tossed in lemon juice instead.

And another area of concern with the fresh fruit is the cooking time. Cooking time would depend on the desired tenderness of the fruit filling when the pie is done. To achieve the desired final consistency, apples should be tender enough when the crust starts to brown. If apple pieces are not tender, cover the pie with foil and cook until tender and juicy, and the crust is golden brown.

Once you know the basic techniques of any recipe, it is very easy to get creative and use different ingredients for desired tastes and fun.

Apple Crumble Pie

Apple crumble pie is a dream dessert. It is delicious served with ice cream, cheddar chunks, or whipped cream. And it is a breeze to make crust.

Single-crust pie recipe (page 25)
Sugar Crumb topping recipe (page 43)
Filling:
6 large apples of your choice (Fuji or Cortland are recommended), peeled, cored, and cut into ½ inch chunks
Juice of 1 lemon
2 tablespoons all-purpose flour
2 tablespoons granulated sugar
¼ teaspoon salt
1 teaspoon cinnamon
½ teaspoon nutmeg grated
2 tablespoons butter, cut into a dice

To make apple pie filling, peel, core, and slice apples. To keep the apples from browning toss in lemon juice instead of soaking in acidulated water. Because, when apples are soaked in water they absorb a lot of water which then exudes during cooking making the filling very wet.

In a small bowl combine the flour, sugar, salt, cinnamon, and nutmeg. Sprinkle the mixture over the apple slices and toss to coat well. Microwave the spiced apples for 20 minutes stirring on and off. Let it cool and then transfer it to the prepared pie shell. Scatter cubed butter over the surface.

Sprinkle the crumb topping mixture evenly over the filling until the filling is fully covered. Bake for 35 to 45 minutes, or until crust is golden and filling is well cooked. Cool completely on a wire rack before serving.

Serve with ice cream of your choice.

Apple Tartlets

A fun dessert to make for entertaining. A puff pastry case filled with diced apples cooked in caramel until deliciously tender. One is just right for one serving.

2 tablespoons unsalted butter
2 tablespoons granulated sugar
2 teaspoons plus a dash of lemon juice
2 Cortland apples, peeled, cored, and cut into small dice
1 sheet puff pastry, thawed and cut into 6 (3-inch) rounds
2 tablespoons Apple jelly
2 teaspoon water
2 tablespoons powdered sugar

- Preheat the oven to 425° F.
- Toss the diced apple with 2 teaspoons lemon juice and set it aside.
- Heat a non-stick saucepan and add 2 tablespoons butter to melt. Once the butter starts melting add 2 tablespoons of granulated sugar. Cook stirring constantly to caramelize the sugar. While stirring, add a dash of lemon juice and continue to cook until sugar caramelizes.
- Drain diced apple and add to the sugar and cook stirring on low heat until apples are quite tender and all the extra water evaporates.
- Remove from heat and bring the apple filling to room temperature.
- Using a 3-inch cookie cutter with a sharp edge, cut out 6 rounds from one puff pastry sheet. Make sure to cut straight down without twisting. Twisting action prevents the edges from rising.
- Mound the apple filling in the center of each round leaving a ¼-inch border-free.
- Arrange all the rounds with filling on a cookie sheet
- Place the cookie sheet in the oven and bake for 20 minutes.
- Meanwhile, heat apple jelly and water in a microwave until it liquefies. Stir

to a smooth consistency and set aside. Use to glaze the tarts.

- Remove the tarts from the oven and let them cool slightly. Apply the glaze to each tart with a pastry brush.

Traditional Apple pie

This pie needs no introduction or recipe since everyone makes it and is well versed in making this delicious dessert.

Crust:

Double-crust pie pastry recipe (page 24)

Filling:

4 granny smith apples, peeled, cored, chopped into small cubes. Put the prepared apple in a bowl along with one tablespoon lemon juice and one tablespoon sugar and give it a toss. set them aside.

1 teaspoon lemon zest

¾ cup sugar plus 1 tablespoon to sprinkle on top

¼ cup all-purpose flour

1 teaspoon kosher salt

¾ teaspoon ground cinnamon

¼ teaspoon ground nutmeg

1 tablespoon plain breadcrumbs

1 egg beaten with 1 tablespoon water for egg wash

- To make the apple pie filling, drain diced apples well to remove all the excess juice.
- Combine apples, ¾ cup sugar, flour, salt, cinnamon, and nutmeg in a bowl.
- Roll out half of the double-crust pie dough. Sprinkle half of the breadcrumbs in the bottom of the 9-inch pie plate, and line it with a rolled-out pastry crust. Sprinkle the remaining half of the crumbs in the pastry shell and press lightly with the bottom of a measuring cup, and chill for 10 to 15 minutes.
- Remove from the refrigerator and transfer the prepared filling into the pastry shell.
- Top with the other half of the rolled-out crust, press the edges, and crimp

the top and bottom to secure the edges.

- Brush with egg wash and sprinkle with sugar. Make a few slashes in the top pastry for the steam to escape.
- place the pie pan in a preheated 350° F. oven and bake for 1 hour and 15 minutes.
- Remove and let it cool on a rack for, at least, 1 hour before serving.
- Can be served with ice cream, whipped cream, or just chunks of cheddar cheese. Sprinkle powdered sugar on each portion to serve.

Mississippi Mud Pie

Crust:
Chocolate graham cracker crust recipe (page 39)
Filling:
2/3 cup sugar
1/3 cup unsweetened cocoa powder
¼ cup cornstarch
¼ teaspoon salt
2½ cups whole milk
4 large egg yolks
1 teaspoon vanilla extract
3-ounce milk chocolate, finely chopped
2 tablespoons unsalted butter, cut into small cubes
Topping:
1 cup heavy cream
2 teaspoons vanilla extract
2 tablespoons sugar
¼ cup chopped pecans

- Combine sugar, cocoa powder, cornstarch, and salt, in a saucepan. Start adding milk slowly while stirring continuously. When well combined, cook on medium heat stirring until it bubbles and is thick.
- In another bowl, whisk egg yolks until smooth. Start adding hot milk mixture in small amounts while stirring vigorously to temper the egg yolks. And then return all the egg mixture to the milk sauce and bring it to a boil, reduce heat and simmer for 2 to 3 minutes. Remove from heat.
- Add the vanilla extract, chopped milk chocolate, and then the butter piece by piece until thoroughly combined.
- Strain the chocolate batter through a sieve into the prepared cooled crust and cover with a plastic sheet and refrigerate overnight. When well set, serve with whipped cream.

- To make the whipped cream topping, beat cream until it starts to get frothy, add vanilla and continue beating while adding sugar in a very slow stream until stiff peaks form. Spread whipped cream as a top layer, and sprinkle chopped pecans on top to Serve.

Classic Pumpkin Pie

Crust:

Single-crust pie pastry recipe (page 25)

Filling:

1 (15 ounces) can pumpkin, or 1 cup freshly processed pumpkin
1 tablespoon corn starch
¾ cup sugar
½ teaspoon ground cinnamon
¼ teaspoon ground ginger
pinch ground nutmeg
½ teaspoon salt.
3 large eggs
¼ cup evaporated milk
¼ cup whole milk
1 tablespoon breadcrumbs

- In a large mixing bowl combine pumpkin, corn starch, sugar, cinnamon, ginger, nutmeg, and salt
- In another bowl, add eggs, evaporated milk, and whole milk and beat lightly with a fork to blend.
- Add it to the pumpkin mixture and mix well.
- Sprinkle half of the breadcrumbs in the bottom of the 9-inch pie plate and line it with a single crust pastry. Sprinkle the remaining half of the crumbs in the pastry shell and press lightly with the bottom of a measuring cup. Transfer the pumpkin filling into the pastry-lined plate.
- Crimp the edges, brush with egg wash, and cover the edges with foil. Bake in a 375° F. oven for 30 minutes.
- Remove foil, lower the heat to 350° F. and bake for 30 minutes more or until a knife inserted off the center comes out clean.
- Remove from the oven, cool, and refrigerate.
- Serve with whipped cream.

Pecan Pie

Pecan pie is one of the easiest pies to make. It is popular throughout the year as opposed to the pumpkin pie which is only popular during the holiday season.

Crust:
Single-crust pie pastry recipe (page 25)
1 tablespoon plain breadcrumbs
Filling:
3 eggs
2/3-cup sugar
2 scant tablespoons all-purpose flour
Dash salt
1 cup dark corn syrup
4 tablespoons butter, melted
1 cup pecan halves
1 egg beaten with 1 tablespoon water for egg wash

- Sprinkle half of the breadcrumbs in the bottom of the 9-inch pie plate and line it with a single crust pastry. Sprinkle the remaining half of the crumbs in the pastry shell and press lightly with the bottom of a measuring cup. Refrigerate while getting the filling ready.
- In a mixing bowl beat eggs with a fork or an eggbeater. Add sugar, flour, salt, corn syrup, and melted butter, mix well to dissolve the sugar.
- Pour the filling into the prepared crust and arrange pecans halves on top of the filling in the desired pattern.
- Crimp the edges, brush with egg wash, and bake in a 350° F. oven for 45 to 50 minutes, or until the knife inserted in the center comes out clean.
- Remove from the oven and let it cool before cutting into it to serve.

Strawberry Rhubarb Pie

It is important to macerate these fruits before the actual cooking. Tossing in sugar makes the fruit release some extra juice. It not only cuts the cooking and thickening time but also enhances the taste, texture, and flavor.

Crust:
Double-crust pie pastry recipe (page 24)
Filling:
3 cups peeled, and diced Rhubarb
1 cup stemmed and quartered strawberries,
1 cup sugar
½ cup quick-cooking tapioca
¼ teaspoon salt
1 teaspoon orange zest
1 egg, and 1 tablespoon water for egg wash

- Preheat the oven to 400° F.
- Rhubarb is very tart, and it is best to toss the diced rhubarb and strawberries with ¼ cup sugar and let the fruit macerate for 20 minutes. This will break down the fruit and release some of the liquid which helps reduce the amount of thickener you need.
- Roll out half of the double-crust pie dough and line a pie plate to prepare the pie shell. Sprinkle breadcrumbs in the shell evenly and chill for 10 to 15 minutes.
- Drain and toss the fruit with the remaining ¾ cup sugar, tapioca, salt, and orange zest in a bowl. Transfer it into the prepared pie shell. Brush the edges with egg wash. Top by rolling another half of the double-crust dough, press the edges, and crimp the top and bottom to secure the edges.
- Cut a few slits with a knife to let the steam escape. Brush the top with egg

wash. Chill for 10 minutes and brush with egg wash a second time before baking. Bake in a 400° F oven for 10 minutes. Lower heat and bake at 350° F. for another 50 - 55 minutes. Cover the edges of the pastry with foil or pastry guard to prevent the edges from over-browning. Remove from the oven to a rack. Refrigerate to cool completely. Serve with ice cream.

Banana Cream Pie

Pastry for 9-inch pie
Filling:
½ cup granulated sugar
¼ cup cornstarch
¼ teaspoon coarse salt
2 cups milk
4 large egg yolks
2 tablespoons cold unsalted butter, cut into pieces
3 ripe bananas, halved lengthwise, thinly sliced crosswise
1 ½ cups heavy cream
2 tablespoons powdered sugar
½ teaspoon pure vanilla extract
Chocolate curls, for garnish

- preheat oven to 450° F.
- Line a 9-inch pie-plate with rolled single crust pastry recipe (page 21).
- Line the top of the pastry with foil and fill with beans for weight. Blind bake for10 minutes. Remove from the oven and take out beans, and the foil. Replace in the oven for 5 to 7 more minutes to get the pastry to brown. Remove from the oven, and let it cool.
- In a medium saucepan, combine granulated sugar, cornstarch, and salt.
- Add milk and whisk until dissolved and smooth mixture forms.
- Cook on medium to high heat whisking continuously until it is bubbling and thick. It will take about 7 minutes (about 2 minutes after it comes to a boil).
- Whisk eggs in a medium bowl, and then add some hot milk mixture in a very slow stream to temper, and to prevent eggs from scrambling.
- Return egg mixture to the milk saucepan and cook stirring continuously until it returns to a boil. About 2 minutes.
- Strain the milk mixture through a fine sieve. Add butter and continue to

stir until all the butter is melted.

- Fold in the banana slices.
- Pour into the prepared crust. Press plastic wrap directly on the surface. Refrigerate overnight.
- In a chilled bowl, beat together cream, powdered sugar, and vanilla until soft peaks form. Spread whipped cream over the filling.
- Using a spatula shape the cream into peaks. Garnish with chocolate curls and serve immediately.

Blueberry Pie

Blueberry pie is Maine's designated state dessert since 2011. But for many years before that, we went to Maine to eat blueberry pie. I have started making blueberry pie because we like it so much, and also it became a big hit with all the kids in my family. Blueberry tart, blueberry crumble, blueberry muffins, and blueberry cobbler are all the other things that became my family favorites and are easy to make and enjoy.

Crust:

2½ cups all-purpose flour
2 tablespoons sugar
½ teaspoon salt
12 tablespoons cold butter, cut into ¼ inch cubes
1/3 cup cold Crisco or vegetable shortening, cut into cubes
2 tablespoons water
¼ cup vodka, a secret ingredient that prevents gluten formation giving you a tender dough.

Filling:

1 cup fresh blueberries
1 can (22 ounces) blueberry filling
2 tablespoons tapioca
¾ cup sugar
1 fresh Cortland apple or any on hand, grated
1 teaspoon lemon zest
pinch salt
2 tablespoons butter, cubed

- Put 1½ cups all-purpose flour, 2 tablespoons sugar, and ½ teaspoon salt, cold cubed butter, and Crisco in a food processor and process until it resembles breadcrumbs.
- Add remaining 1 cup flour, and add water and vodka and give 6 to 8

pulses.

- Transfer the contents of the food processor to a work surface.
- It will look a little too wet but don't add more flour. Divide it into two halves and form into balls and wrap in a plastic wrap and chill for 45 minutes. It can be done 2 days ahead of time.
- When ready to bake, roll out one half to fit a pie plate with an overhang of about 3 inches. Cover with plastic wrap and refrigerate until the filling is ready.
- Cook down 1 cup of fresh blueberries to a jam consistency by mashing them with a potato masher.
- Transfer to a large mixing bowl, and add the can of blueberry filling, and stir to mix. Add tapioca, sugar, grated apple, zest, and salt. Mix to incorporate,
- Transfer the filling to the pastry shell-lined pie plate and scatter butter cubes on top.
- Roll out the other half of the dough for the top. Cover the filling. Seal well and crimp the edges.
- Brush with egg wash and bake at 350° F. preheated oven for an hour until golden brown.
- Transfer to a cooling rack and let it cool for 2 hours before cutting into it.

Shoofly Pie

Paté Brisée pastry crust recipe (page 27)

Filling:

1 teaspoon baking soda

¾ cup molasses

¾ cup hot water

1 cup all-purpose flour

2/3 cup brown sugar, firmly packed

2 tablespoons cold, unsalted butter, cubed

1 large egg, beaten

1 teaspoon vanilla

- Preheat oven to 400° F.
- Roll out the refrigerated dough to fit a 9 ½ inch pie plate. Line the plate and press firmly against the bottom and sides. Crimp the edges and refrigerate until ready to use.
- Stir baking soda and molasses with hot water until well blended and set aside.
- In a bowl, whisk in flour and brown sugar. Cut the butter into the mixture until it resembles coarse crumbs.
- Remove and reserve ½ cup of crumb mixture in a separate bowl.
- Add beaten egg, and vanilla to molasses mixture and stir to blend thoroughly. Pour the liquid into the flour, sugar, and butter crumb mixture.
- Beat to get a smooth batter. Pour the batter into the prepared pie shell.
- Sprinkle with the reserved crumb mixture and bake for 10 minutes.
- Reduce oven heat to 350° F. and bake for 50 minutes or until filling is set.
- Serve warm with whipped cream or your choice of ice cream.

Cherry Pie

For cherry pie all you need to do is mix filling ingredients and fill the prepared pie shell and bake. But a lot of home bakers are fearful of making crust at home. The recipes in this book are designed to bake with understanding which leads to success.

Crust:

Double-crust pie pastry recipe (Page 24)

Filling:

1 can (15 ounces) cherry pie filling

6-ounce cherries pitted, washed, and drained

1 cup sugar

¼ cup tapioca, ground

1 teaspoon vanilla extract

1 tablespoon plain breadcrumbs

2 tablespoon unsalted, cubed butter for topping

1 egg lightly beaten

1 tablespoon sugar

- preheat oven to 375° F.
- Mix pie filling, fresh cherries, sugar, tapioca, and vanilla extract in a large bowl and set it aside.
- Sprinkle half of the breadcrumbs in the bottom of the 9-inch pie plate and line it with half of the rolled-out pastry crust. Sprinkle the remaining half of the crumbs in the pastry shell and press lightly with the bottom of a measuring cup. Refrigerate for 15 to 20 minutes. The warm crust would collapse in a hot oven.
- Add the prepared filling and spread it evenly. Scatter butter cubes on top of the filling and brush the edges with the beaten egg. Top it with another half of the rolled-out pie crust. Press the edges together to seal and crimp. Cut some holes with a mini round cookie cutter in the top

crust to allow the steam to escape. Brush with egg wash, sprinkle with sugar.

- Bake in a preheated oven for 10 minutes, then turn the heat down to 350° F. and bake for 50 minutes or until golden brown with the bubbling of the cherry filling. Let it cool before cutting into it.

Lemon Meringue Pie

To make the meringue, separate eggs with great care. Even a trace of yellow in the white will prevent whites to work. It is also important that the bowl and the whisk are meticulously clean and cold. Place the bowl and whisk in the freezer for 10 to 15 minutes to get them cold.

4 egg yolks
4 egg whites for meringue
pinch cream of tartar
1/3 cup cornstarch
1 ½ cups water
1 1/3 cups sugar
¼ teaspoon salt
3 tablespoons butter
½ cup fresh lemon juice
2 teaspoons finely grated lemon zest

- Cook the store-bought pie shell and precook it in a 400° F. oven for 15 minutes. And set aside to cool.
- Reheat the oven to 375° F. with the rack in the center of the oven.
- In a very clean bowl of a stand mixer, add 4 egg whites and pinch cream of tartar and whisk until soft peak stage. Start adding sugar in a very slow stream and continue to beat to stiff peak stage (2 minutes). Set it in the refrigerator to use for topping the pie.
- In a medium bowl, whisk egg yolks until they are pale yellow and well whisked. Set aside.
- Add cornstarch, water, sugar, and salt to a saucepan and stir to combine thoroughly. Place it on medium heat and bring it to a boil until it is thick and shiny. Remove from heat and add small amounts into the beaten eggs to temper and prevent scrambling. When the temperature of the egg yolk has risen enough, add the mixture to the original pot and cook on

low heat stirring gently.

- Remove from heat and stir in butter, lemon juice, and zest until evenly mixed. Return to the heat and continue simmering while stirring until the added liquid gets well incorporated and the mixture is fairly thick.
- Transfer the mixture into the precooked, and cooled pie shell, and immediately top with prepared meringue and use a spatula to cover the filling properly and also making sure to seal the edges by bringing meringue right to the crust.
- This is an important step and should be done quickly to prevent filling from cooling down. Because the heat of the filling helps to cook the meringue.
- Bake in a preheated oven for 12-15 minutes until meringue is golden.
- Transfer to a wire rack for the pie to cool completely before serving.

Chocolate Peanut Butter Tart

For the Crust

8 oz. (about 40 cookies) Nabisco Chocolate Wafers, finely ground
¼ cup sugar
6 tablespoons unsalted butter, melted
pinch salt

For the Peanut Butter Filling

6 tablespoons butter, cut in a dice
3 tablespoons heavy cream
¾ cup creamy peanut butter
½ teaspoon vanilla extract
Pinch of salt
1 ¼ cup confectioner sugar, sifted

For the Ganache

10 oz. semisweet chocolate, finely chopped
1 tablespoon unsalted butter, room temperature
1 ¼ cup heavy cream

For the Garnish

¼ cup salted roasted peanuts, chopped

Place Nabisco crackers into a food processor and process until they resemble breadcrumbs. Add sugar, melted butter, and salt and process until it resembles wet sand. Transfer the mixture into a removable bottom 10-inch tart pan and firmly press with a measuring cup in the bottom and up the side of the pan. Bake in a 350° F. oven for 15 minutes. Transfer to a wire rack and let it cool completely.

For the Filling

Combine butter, cream, peanut butter, vanilla, and salt in a saucepan over medium heat and cook until everything is melted into a smooth sauce. Pour over sifted confectioner sugar and whisk to a smooth, thick sauce. Pour into the cooled crust, tightly cover with a plastic wrap and refrigerate until it sets.

For the Topping

Place chocolate and butter in a heat-proof bowl. Bring the cream to a simmering boil and pour over the chocolate mixture. Let it stand for 5 minutes until chocolate melts, and then use a spatula to stir until it is emulsified. Set it aside to cool for about 30 minutes. At this point, the ganache should be thick, glossy, and yet pourable.

Place the tart on a revolving cake stand. Pour ganache into the center. Use an offset spatula to spread the ganache while rotating the cake stand until the ganache comes just shy of the edges. Garnish with chopped, salted roasted peanuts. Let it sit for about 1 hour before cutting into it.

Blueberry Tart

Make sure to bring the cream cheese to room temperature. And it is imperative to put the bowl and whisk in the freezer to get them cold to get the whipped cream to stiff peaks stage. Also do not mix the whipped cream mixture with cream cheese vigorously. Folding action is important to get the required consistency.

Crust:
½ cup powdered sugar
1½ cups all-purpose flour
¾ cup (1½ sticks) butter, softened
½ cup finely chopped pecans, or your favorite type of nuts
Filling:
1 can (22 ounces) blueberry pie filling
½ cup granulated sugar
1 tablespoon fresh lemon juice
Pinch grated nutmeg
2 (3 ounces) packages of cream cheese, at room temperature
1 cup powdered sugar
1 cup heavy cream
¼ cup sugar

- Preheat oven to 350° F.
- In a bowl, stir together blueberries from the can, ½ cup granulated sugar, lemon juice, and nutmeg. Set it aside.
- Crust:
- Use a food processor to make the dough by pulsing powdered sugar, flour, and butter until the mixture forms a ball. Transfer dough to a tart pan with a removable bottom and firmly press the dough in the bottom and grooves of the tart pan with the help of a small measuring cup. Sprinkle the chopped pecans into the crust and press evenly. Bake for 10-12

minutes until lightly browned. Let it cool before filling.

- Filling:
- In a bowl beat room temperature cream cheese with powdered sugar with a hand mixer until really smooth. Meanwhile, in a stand mixer bowl beat heavy cream with sugar until stiff peaks form.
- Add whipped cream to the cream cheese mixture and mix with folding action to make sure not to lose the air incorporated during whipping. Transfer it to the cooled pie shell and level with an offset spatula thoroughly and neatly.
- Top it with the prepared blueberry pie filling.
- Place it in the refrigerator until well chilled, at least, 2-3 hours. It is even better to chill it overnight.
- Cut wedges and serve with whipped cream, ice-cream, or as is.

Cranberry Tart

Cranberry tart is beautiful in that it looks like it is studded with precious rubies. Flakey crust easily breaks with a fork, and its tart taste requires that it be served with fresh whipped cream or ice cream.

Crust:
¾ cup finely chopped, walnuts
6 tablespoons unsalted butter, room temperature
1 large egg
1 teaspoon vanilla
2 tablespoons sugar
1 cup bleached all-purpose flour
Filling:
2 packets gelatin
½ cup water
6 cups cranberries
1 cup red currant jelly
2 cups sugar

- Put the chopped walnuts in a bowl of a stand mixer. Add butter, 1 egg, and vanilla. Mix until well combined.
- Add sugar, and flour and continue mixing until the dough comes together.
- Transfer to a 9 x 6 - inch tart pan with a removable bottom. Press the dough evenly with fingers or with the bottom of a measuring cup bringing the dough up the sides. Refrigerate for 30 minutes.
- Once it is chilled, pre-bake the tart shell in a preheated 375° F. oven for 15 to 20 minutes, or until golden brown.
- In a bowl add gelatin and ½ cup water and stir to dissolve gelatin thoroughly.
- Meanwhile, in a saucepan, add cranberries, red currant jelly, and sugar. Cook the mixture stirring a few times until cranberries are soft but not

bruised. Let the mixture cool slightly and then stir in gelatin mixture. Let the filling cool completely.

- Pour cranberry filling into the tart shell and refrigerate overnight before serving. Serve with whipped cream.

Bakewell Tart

This tart is elegant, delicious, and quite easy to make dessert. It is a treat your guest will love.

Crust:
- ¾ cup (1½ stick) chilled, unsalted butter, cut into small cubes
- 2/3 cup sugar
- pinch salt
- 1 teaspoon vanilla extract
- 2 egg yolks
- 2 cups flour

Filling:
- enough cherry, raspberry, or your choice jam
- Frangipani, recipe follows (page 74)

For Glaze:
- 1 cup powdered sugar
- 1 tablespoon fresh lemon juice

- Add chilled butter, and 2/3 cup sugar to the bowl of a food processor, and process until combined.
- Add salt, vanilla extract, 2 egg yolks, and process again.
- Add flour 1 cup at a time and process to form the dough.
- Remove the dough to a plastic wrap and press to form a smooth disc using the wrap without touching the dough. Chill the dough for, at least, 30 minutes.
- Roll the dough out to 1/8-inch thickness and line a 9-inch removable bottom tart pan with the pastry, and press in the bottom and into the fluted edges. Smooth the edges by cutting out the overhang. While working the dough will soften slightly, therefore, it is better to refrigerate for 20 minutes to firm it up.
- When ready, spread 1 cup of well-stirred jam in the bottom smoothly. And

then add prepared frangipane on top and smooth it out.

- place the tart pans on a baking sheet, and bake in a preheated 350-degree oven for 30-35 minutes. If it starts to over-brown, cover with foil until it bakes for the required amount of time. Remove and bring it to room temperature.
- To make the glaze, sift 1 cup powdered sugar to remove the lumps.
- Mix sifted sugar, and fresh lemon juice and stir it up to make a smooth glaze. squiggle over the tart to serve.

Frangipane

Frangipane is a cream filling made from nuts, sugar, eggs, and flour. It is used in tarts and pastries. Bostock and Bakewell's tarts are some of the varieties made with frangipani. It is similar to the custard-filled tart but was used traditionally for desserts made for the Christmas celebration.

2/3 cup almonds, lightly toasted
½ cup sugar
¾ teaspoon salt
½ teaspoon almond extract
6 tablespoons butter, room temperature
1 large egg
2 tablespoons flour
1 tablespoon rum (optional)

- Toast almonds lightly, making sure not to burn.
- In a food processor, grind toasted almonds, and sugar until a very fine powder.
- Add teaspoon salt, ½ teaspoon almond extract, 6 tablespoons room temperature butter, 1 large egg, 2 tablespoons all-purpose flour, and 1 tablespoon rum if using.
- Process the mixture until it becomes a paste.
- It can be used for various recipes, and also can be frozen for later use.

Fresh oranges and Yogurt Tart

Easy and elegant dessert and worth making for any party. It is simple, economical, pretty, and delicious.

Crust:
- ½ cup raw almonds
- ¼ cup granulated sugar
- ½ teaspoon coarse salt
- 1 cup all-purpose flour
- 6 tablespoons cold, unsalted butter, cut into cubes
- 1 large egg

Filling:
- 2 teaspoons unflavored powdered gelatin
- 2 tablespoons ice water
- ½ cup whole milk
- 1½ cup plain Greek-style yogurt
- ¼ cup packed light brown sugar
- pinch coarse salt
- 3 navel oranges

- Preheat the oven to 350° F.
- To make the crust, Process almonds, granulated sugar, and salt in a food processor until finely ground. Add flour and process. Then add cubed, cold butter and process until it resembles breadcrumbs. Break in the egg and pulse until the mixture comes together to form a soft dough. Transfer to a 9-inch tart pan and press with the bottom of a measuring cup until the bottom and sides of the tart pan are firmly lined.
- Bake in 350° F. oven for 15 minutes and let it cool completely on a wire rack.
- In a small bowl, sprinkle gelatin over water and let it stand for it to soften. Meanwhile, pour the milk into a saucepan and bring it to a simmer. When

the milk steams, add gelatin mixture and stir to dissolve thoroughly.

- In another bowl mix yogurt, with brown sugar and salt by whisking. Slowly whisk in the warm milk into the yogurt mixture until well combined. Pour the filling into the prepared tart shell and smooth it with an offset spatula. Cover with plastic wrap and refrigerate overnight for it to set.
- Slice the ends of the oranges and peel making sure that you remove as much white pith as you can. Cut into ¼ -inch thick slices and discard the seeds. Arrange on a platter and cover with plastic wrap. When ready to serve, arrange orange slices on top of the tart.
- Cut into wedges to serve.

Fresh Fruit Tart

This stunning dessert is one of the most popular. Its tender, crispy, and yet not too crumbly pastry is awe-inspiring. The custard layer with its shiny glazed beautiful berries is mouthwatering and delicious.

Crust:
- ½ cup chopped almonds or pecans
- 1¼ cup all-purpose flour
- ¼ cup dark brown sugar
- pinch salt
- 1 egg
- 4 tablespoons unsalted butter
- Pastry Cream; recipe (page142)

Fruit Toppings:
- 1 cup blueberries
- ½ pound strawberries stemmed and halved
- 2 or 3 kiwis, peeled and thinly sliced

Glaze:
- ¼ cup apricot preserve

- Preheat the oven to 375° F.
- In a food processor, process nuts of your choice until they resemble fine breadcrumbs.
- Add flour, brown sugar, and salt, and pulse to combine everything. Add egg and butter and process until it resembles wet sand.
- Transfer the mixture to a tart pan with removable bottom and press to make a crust of ¼ thickness extending ½ inch up the sides of the tart pan.
- Bake the crust in a 375° F. oven for 15 minutes. When ready remove from the oven and cool to room temperature.
- Meanwhile, prepare the glaze by heating apricot jam in a small saucepan.

cook stirring until it thins slightly, then strain it through a medium-mesh sieve, use the liquid as a glaze and discard the solids.

- When ready to assemble, pour cooled pastry cream on top of the prepared crust and smooth it out evenly with an offset spatula.
- Arrange berries in the desired design and brush all the fruits generously with the glaze and refrigerate for at least 30 minutes before cutting into it.
- Great-looking and tasting variations are easy to do. I have done fresh mango tart with great success. Its stunning looks are highly tempting, and the taste is just simply delectable and memorable.

Almonds or Pistachios Nut Tart

This recipe is from Martha Stewart's "Marth Bakes". I made it over and over again with no problems. Everyone who eats it has nothing but 'wow' for it!

Crust:
¾ cup all-purpose flour
¼ cup cocoa powder
¼ teaspoon salt
1/3 cup finely chopped almonds or Pistachios
1 stick softened butter
¼ cup sugar
½ teaspoon vanilla
For a layer of groundnuts:
½ cup almonds or pistachios, ground in a food processor
¼ teaspoon salt
1 teaspoon oil (canola oil)
¼ cup sugar
For the chocolate filling:
5-ounce milk chocolate
½ cup heavy cream
¼ cup milk, heated
1 large egg, lightly beaten
Garnish:
½ cup very finely chopped nuts for embellishment

- In a bowl, whisk ¾ cup all-purpose flour, ¼ cup cocoa powder, ¼ teaspoon salt, 1/3 cup finely chopped nuts of your choice until combined.
- In a bowl of a standing mixer with a paddle attachment, beat 1 stick (½ cup) softened butter, ¼ cup sugar, and ½ teaspoon vanilla.
- Add the dry ingredients and continue to beat until it all comes together.

Transfer the dough to a plastic wrap, and make sure to scrape the bowl clean. You can bring all the dough into a ball and then into a disc with the help of plastic wrap without touching it. Wrap and refrigerate for, at least, 30 minutes.

- When ready, flour a piece of plastic wrap and put the dough disc on top. Flour the top of the dough and again cover with another piece of plastic wrap to roll the dough between the two plastic sheets to fit a 9-inch tart pan. Working quickly is important to keep the dough from becoming too soft. If it gets soft chill it until it is firm.
- Remove the top layer of plastic and put the removable bottom of the tart pan on top of the rolled crust. Invert the pastry with great care in the tart pan removing the plastic sheet gently from the top. Ease the pastry in the pan and fold the overhang in on itself with the help of flour on your hands, and push the pastry into the grooves of the tart pan. Return to the refrigerator to chill for 30 minutes. When it is chilled bake in a 325° F. oven for 30 minutes. Let it cool before filling.
- Meanwhile, in a food processor, grind nuts, ¼ teaspoon salt, and 1 teaspoon flavorless oil until it is almost a paste. And then add ¼ cup sugar and process until well blended.
- Put the mixture in the prepared tart shell and even it out on the bottom and press with the bottom of the measuring cup to create a firm layer.
- Meanwhile, in a saucepan, mix 5-ounce milk chocolate, ½ cup heavy cream, and ¼ cup milk and heat until it starts to bubble. let it sit for a few minutes.
- Whisk melted chocolate, and 1 beaten egg thoroughly. Pour it onto the nut base.
- Bake in a 300° F. preheated oven for 30 to 35 minutes.
- By carefully removing the tart ring, place the tart along with the tart pan bottom on a serving platter.
- By using chopped nuts, decorate the tart. Refrigerate for one or two hours. Cut wedges and serve with whipped cream.

Lemon and Lime Tart

½ cup freshly squeezed lemon and lime juice
1½ sleeve of saltine crackers
3 tablespoons light brown sugar
½ cup unsalted butter softened
1 can (14 ounces) sweetened condensed milk
4 egg yolks
1 teaspoon sea salt
Whipped cream for topping (recipe page 139)

- In a food processor, pulse crackers to make crumbs. Make sure to avoid pulsing to a fine powder. Add brown sugar and pulse. Add softened butter and mix to combine. Transfer to a work surface and knead so the crumbs hold like dough.
- Transfer to an 8-inch removable bottom tart pan and press it firmly in the bottom and around the fluted edge for a firm finish. You can use a small measuring cup to help to press the crumbs in.
- Chill the shell for 15 minutes. Bake for 15 to 20 minutes. Let it cool completely.
- Squeezed fresh lemons and limes to get ½ cup juice and set aside.
- In a bowl, pour all the condensed milk by scraping it all around the can and the bottom to get all of it out without waste.
- Separate egg yolk and whites very carefully. Save the egg whites for some other use. Add four yolks to the condensed milk and beat to thoroughly combine.
- Add freshly squeezed lemon-lime juice and beat to combine.
- Pour into the cooled tart shell. Bake at 350° F. preheated oven for 20 to 25 minutes or until the pie is well set. Transfer to a rack and sprinkle with sea salt. Cool before serving
- Top it with freshly whipped cream.

Pineapple Upside-Down Cake

Yellow pineapple rings and red cherries make this cake mouthwatering delicious. The easy availability of all the ingredients, adds to its appeal.

Glaze:

½ cup packed brown sugar
8 tablespoons (1 stick) unsalted butter
pinch salt
Cake Batter:
1 stick butter, softened
1 cup sugar
1 teaspoon vanilla extract
2 eggs
1 ¼ cups cake flour
pinch salt
1 ¾ teaspoons baking powder
2/3 cup whole milk
6 pineapple slices
6 maraschino cherries
6 ramekins, well-greased
Caramel:
¾ cup sugar
¼ cup water
1 cup heavy cream
1 teaspoon vanilla extract
1 tablespoon rum (optional)
1 tablespoon butter

- Put brown sugar, butter, and salt in a small saucepan and cook until fairly thick and turns into a smooth glaze.
- In a bowl of a stand mixer, cream butter and sugar until fully combined.

Add vanilla and eggs and beat until smooth.

- In another bowl, whisk cake flour, salt, and baking powder.
- Start adding dry ingredients and milk alternatively to the egg mixture while beating until smooth.
- Put one tablespoon of prepared glaze in each ramekin. Put a slice of pineapple on top of the glaze. Put a cherry in the center of each pineapple slice.
- Put 2 tablespoons of batter in each ramekin and arrange in a tray. Add warm water to the tray until it comes halfway up the ramekins. Bake in a preheated oven for 35 minutes.
- If you don't want to do individual ramekins, use a soufflé bowl and follow the same method for assembling by pouring glaze to the bottom completely and then arranging the required number of pineapple slices with a maraschino cherry in the center of each slice. Pour the entire cake batter on top and put the bowl in a tray and bake in a preheated oven for 40 to 45 minutes.
- Meanwhile, add ¾ cup sugar in ¼ cup water and cook until the sugar turns to caramel. Turn the heat off and add 1 cup heavy cream stirring vigorously. Add vanilla, rum (if using), and 1 tablespoon butter to finish.
- Remove the ramekins from the oven and let cool. When cool, run a knife around each one and invert to a serving plate. If you have a whole cake, invert it and then cut it into wedges before pouring the prepared caramel on each serving.

Molten Chocolate Cake

4-ounce semisweet chocolate

8 tablespoons (1 stick) butter

2 eggs plus 2 egg yolks

¼ cup sugar

2 teaspoon flour

Preheat oven to 450° F.

Grease 6 ramekins (4 ounces each) and generously flour them to prevent cakes from sticking.

- Melt chocolate and butter in a microwave on high for 30 seconds. Remove and stir. Repeat heating at shorter intervals until chocolate melts completely and has a smooth consistency.
- In a bowl of a stand mixer, whip 2 eggs and 2-egg yolks with ¼ cup sugar until light, and fluffy.
- Add 2-teaspoon flour and whip to mix thoroughly.
- Pour melted chocolate into the egg mixture and whip to combine.
- Pour equal amounts in 6 (4 ounces each) prepared ramekins.
- Bake in a preheated oven for 7 to 8 minutes
- Serve with a dollop of whipped cream.
- This is a good dessert for entertaining. You can pour the prepared chocolate into the ramekins and keep it in the refrigerator until just before serving. Bake for 7 to 8 minutes in a preheated 450° F. oven. Remove from the oven, and garnish with glazed berries (optional).
- Serve with whipped cream.

Angel Food Cake

1 cup sifted cake flour
1 cup superfine sugar, divided
1½ cups egg whites (10-12 eggs), room temperature
1 teaspoon cream of tartar
¼ teaspoon salt
2 teaspoons vanilla extract
½ teaspoon almond extract

- Preheat oven to 325° F.
- Combine flour and ¼ cup sugar in a bowl and set it aside.
- Beat egg whites until frothy, and then add cream of tartar and salt. Beat until fully incorporated then start adding the remaining ¾ cup sugar in 2 tablespoons portions at a time until all the sugar is added. When sugar is added, beat egg whites to soft peaks. You will know when it is ready because the egg white will form waves. Add the vanilla and almond extracts and continue to beat for a few seconds to evenly distribute.
- Sift flour and sugar mixture in a bowl, and add to the egg whites in 6 to 8 additions and gently fold it in after each addition.
- Spoon the batter into an ungreased 9-inch tube pan with a removable bottom. Smooth the top with a spatula and tap the pan on the counter to remove any large bubbles in the mixture. Bake for 50 to 60 minutes, until the top springs back when lightly pressed. Allow it to cool overnight.
- Gently run a thin knife around the sides to release the cake when ready to serve.

Pound Cake

Pound cake is a classic cake which is an all-time favorite. It is called pound cake because to make it, one pound each of the basic ingredients such as flour, butter, sugar, and eggs are used. There are several recipes with variations. I developed this recipe after attempting to use slight changes in ingredients, and amounts I used.

4 cups cake flour
4 teaspoon baking powder, fresh
1 teaspoon kosher salt
3 sticks butter, room temperature but not too soft
3 cups sugar
2 teaspoon vanilla
½ teaspoon pure lemon extract
8 fresh large eggs
1 cup milk or heavy cream

- preheat oven to 325° F.
- Well grease and flour bread loaf pan and set aside.
- In a bowl, sift cake flour to remove any lumps it may have.
- Whisk in 4 teaspoon baking powder and 1 teaspoon kosher salt to well combine.
- In a stand mixer with a paddle attachment, cream 3 sticks of softened unsalted butter, and 3 cups sugar until sugar is dissolved. Add vanilla extract, and pure lemon extract and beat. Adding flavoring at this point works well because fat helps distribute the flavor well.
- Start adding eggs one at a time and beat until well incorporated.
- Start adding dry ingredients and milk or heavy cream in small portions alternatively while still whisking. Do it quickly to avoid overbeating.
- Transfer the batter to the prepared loaf pan almost to the top.
- Bake in a preheated oven for 1 hour and 30 minutes.
- Remove from the oven and let it cool slightly before running a knife or an

offset spatula all around and turn it over onto a rack. And turn it to the right side to cool. It most likely will have a crack in the center like quick banana bread. Cut and serve with desired cream and fruits.

Sticky Toffee Pudding

Sticky toffee pudding is a British dessert with the sweetness and special taste derived from dates. Its spongy texture is made juicier by the addition of sauce which is poured over it giving it an extra depth of flavor.

8 ounces pitted dates chopped finely
1¼ cup water
1 teaspoon baking soda
1½ cups sifted all-purpose flour, plus more for the pan
1 teaspoon baking powder
½ teaspoon sea salt
¼ cup (½ stick) unsalted butter, room temperature, plus more for greasing the pan
1 cup sugar
1 teaspoon vanilla extract
2 large eggs
3 tablespoons molasses
Sauce:
¼ cup (½ stick) unsalted butter
1¼ cups packed light brown sugar
½ cup heavy cream
1 tablespoon rum (optional)
½ teaspoon lemon juice

- Preheat the oven to 350-degree F.
- Butter and flour a Bundt pan.
- Bring dates and water to a boil on medium heat in a heavy-bottomed saucepan. Remove from heat and stir in baking soda. Set aside when the mixture becomes foamy.
- Whisk flour, baking powder, and salt in a bowl.
- In a bowl of a stand mixer, cream butter and sugar until sugar is well dissolved, then add vanilla extract and mix.

- Add 1 egg and beat to blend.
- Add half of the flour mixture, molasses, and half of the date mixture and continue to blend.
- Add the remaining egg, the rest of the flour mixture, and the remaining date mixture and beat to blend well.
- Pour into the Bundt pan, until 2/3 full.
- Place the Bundt pan in a roasting pan and then place it in a preheated oven. Pour enough boiling water into the roasting pan to come ¼ inch up to the sides of the Bundt pan.
- Bake until a toothpick inserted in the center of the cake comes out clean, about 45 minutes.
- Remove from the oven and let it cool.

Sauce:

- Cook 4 tablespoon butter and 1¼ cup brown sugar in a saucepan over medium heat, stirring constantly until sugar dissolves and the mixture is slightly darkened.
- Add half of the cream and stir to mix. Add the rest of the cream along with rum (if using) whisking constantly to get a smooth sauce.
- Remove from the heat and stir in lemon juice.
- Pour half the sauce into a serving dish the size of the cake. Invert the cake into the sauce.
- With a kebab skewer make several holes in the cake, and pour the remaining sauce over the cake to soak it thoroughly.
- Cut into wedges. Serve with whipped cream or vanilla ice cream.

Roasted Apples

5 granny smith apples, apples of your choice
2 sticks butter, melted
1- ½ cup sugar
Pinch cinnamon powder
8 ounce heavy cream

- Preheat oven to 375° F.
- Peel, core, and quarter apples. Soak in acidulated water until ready to use.
- Drain and pat dry apples. Spread the prepared apples slices in a large Dutch oven enough in one layer.
- Add butter, and liberally coat with sugar and cinnamon powder.
- Roast apples at 375° F until soft, and caramelized at the bottom with butter floating on the top.
- Remove from the oven and transfer apples to a serving dish with a slotted spoon leaving all the juices in the pan.
- Stir in heavy cream in the juices remaining in the pan and place on medium heat and simmer while stirring with a wooden spoon until the caramel dissolves completely forming thick delicious sauce.
- Strain the sauce and spoon over the apples to serve.

Baked Custards

Making Basic Custard and Pastry Cream:

Custard is one of the most popular desserts. It is made with milk or cream thickened with egg yolks. The dairy provides creamy consistency which is emulsified by egg yolks giving it an irresistible texture.

There are different types of custard. Basic custard is cooked carefully in an evenly heated water bath or a double boiler stirring constantly. While cooking, it is important to use a thermometer to ensure that it is under 180 °F when removed from heat. If it is heated even slightly more it breaks or curdles. Crème brulée and cream anglaize are examples of basic custard.

Pastry cream is a starch thickened custard. Added cornstarch or flour give the pastry cream an extra body. And it is cooked over direct heat. As opposed to basic custard, pastry cream has to come to a simmer and be cooked for 1 or 2 minutes after it starts to bubble. Bringing it to a simmering boil ensures that the Amylase enzyme in the yolk is denatured and rendered inactive. If amylase is still active, it will attack an initially thick pastry cream and turn it into a soupy mess.

When pastry cream in your fruit tart turns thin, it is because it did not cook enough to deactivate the enzyme which causes the problem.

Coconut Flan

½ cup sweetened coconut flakes
½ teaspoon ground cinnamon
1 cup granulated sugar
1 tablespoon water
1(14 ounces) can condensed milk
1 (13.5-ounce) can coconut cream
1 cup (15 ounces) evaporated milk
6 eggs, beaten
1 teaspoon vanilla
½ teaspoon salt

- Preheat oven to 350° F.
- Sprinkle cinnamon over coconut flakes and spread on a rimmed cookie sheet. Toast in the preheated oven until golden brown, about 5 minutes, and set it aside.
- Meanwhile, heat a heavy saucepan on medium-high heat. Add 1-cup of sugar, and 1-tablespoon water to the hot saucepan. Cook until the sugar liquefies and turns into caramel. Turn the burner off and transfer caramel into a 9½ inch pie plate, or a soufflé bowl. Swirl the container to evenly coat with the caramel. It should be done with quick movements to prevent the caramel from hardening before the plate is covered with it.
- In a blender, add condensed milk, coconut cream, evaporated milk, 6 eggs, vanilla, and salt.
- Blend the content until ingredients are thoroughly incorporated.
- Pour the blended mixture into the caramel-lined container.
- Place the pan in a baking tray and put it into the preheated oven.
- Heat water in a kettle and add hot water to the baking tray until the water comes halfway up the sides of the container. Bake in a 350° F. oven for 1 hour and 30 minutes.
- Remove from the oven and let it cool by placing flan on a rack. Once it

comes to room temperature, slide a knife around the edge, and then carefully turn it over onto a serving platter.

- Cover with plastic wrap and place in the refrigerator overnight.
- Remove the flan from the refrigerator and remove the plastic wrap. Top it with a thick layer of toasted coconut flakes.
- Cut into wedges to serve.

Mexican Flan

Flan is a luxurious dessert loved by young and old alike. It is particularly popular in Spain and Latin American countries. Like other desserts, it has many versions. My version is made in a soufflé bowl to give it extra thickness and character. Now is the time to try.

1-cup sugar

1-tablespoon water

1 (7.6-ounces) can of media crèma (you can get this in any supermarket, if not, Wal-Mart has it.

You can substitute Media Crèma with 1(14 ounces) heavy cream

3 eggs

3 egg yolks

1(12 ounces) can of evaporated milk

1 (14 ounces) can condensed milk

1 teaspoon vanilla

¼ teaspoon salt

- Preheat oven to 350° F. Heat a heavy saucepan on medium-high heat. Add 1-cup of sugar, and 1- tablespoon water to the hot saucepan.
- Cook until the sugar liquefies and turns to caramel.
- Turn the burner off and transfer the caramel into a well-greased and floured deep porcelain pie plate, or a soufflé bowl.
- Swirl the container to evenly coat with the caramel. It should be done with quick movements to prevent the caramel from hardening before the bottom is covered with it.
- In a blender, add the media crèma, 3 eggs, 3 yolks, evaporated milk, condensed milk, vanilla, and salt.
- Blend the content until ingredients are thoroughly combined.
- Pour the blended mixture into the caramel-lined pie plate.
- Place the pan in a baking tray and put it into the preheated oven.

- Heat water in a kettle and add hot water to the baking tray until the water comes halfway up the sides of the pie plate.
- Cook in a 350° F. oven for 1 hour and 15 minutes.
- Remove from the oven and let it cool slightly by placing the pie plate on a rack.
- Once it comes to room temperature, slide a knife around the edge, and then carefully invert onto a serving platter.
- Cover with a plastic wrap and place in the refrigerator overnight before serving.

Tres Leches Cake

½ cup softened butter, softened
1 cup sugar
6 room temperature eggs
½ teaspoon vanilla extract
1 ½ cup flour, sifted before measuring
1 teaspoon baking powder
1/4 cup whole milk
1 (14 oz.) can condensed milk
1 (15 oz.) can evaporated milk
whipped cream for topping recipe (page 139)

- Preheat oven to 325° F.
- Sift flour and baking powder well and then measure 1 ½ cups and set aside.
- Grease and flour a 13x9 -inch baking tray and set it aside for use later.
- In a bowl, beat softened butter with one cup of sugar until fluffy.
- Add 6 eggs and ½ teaspoon vanilla extract and beat to mix well.
- Start adding sifted flour to the egg mixture one tablespoon at a time with a hand beater until it is all blended.
- Pour the batter into the prepared baking tray and bake in a preheated 325° F oven for 30 minutes.
- Remove the cake from the oven, and let it cool completely. Once cooled, pierce the cake with a fork all over.
- While the cake is baking, in another bowl whisk together whole milk, condensed milk, and evaporated milk until incorporated. Pour the milk mixture all over the cake.
- Tightly cover with plastic wrap and refrigerate for a few hours or overnight.
- Remove from the refrigerator, and pipe whipped cream in the desired pattern to serve.

Crème Brulées

Crème Brulée is a French, creamy, custardy dessert with a caramelized crispy topping.

4 cups heavy cream
1 cup granulated sugar
pinch salt
8 large egg yolks
2 teaspoon vanilla
enough sugar for topping

- Preheat oven to 350° F. Arrange 8 (6 oz.) ramekins in a baking pan. Adjust the oven rack to the lower third.
- Heat a large kettle of water.
- Meanwhile, in a medium saucepan, combine heavy cream, granulated sugar, and salt. Bring the mixture to a simmering boil (means don't let it get to a rolling boil. When you see bubbles around the edges, it is ready) while stirring to dissolve the sugar.
- Whisk egg yolks until light in color and fluffy, add vanilla and whisk to combine until smooth. Start adding hot cream into the egg mixture in a steady and very slow stream, while stirring vigorously, to prevent eggs from scrambling, until all the cream is incorporated. The mixture should lightly coat the back of the spoon.
- Strain through a fine-mesh sieve into a large liquid measuring cup and discard the solids.
- Pour an even amount of mixture into each of the ramekins.
- Transfer the baking pan to the oven and pour hot water into it until it reaches halfway up the side of the ramekin.
- Bake the custard for 30 to 40 minutes in 350° F. preheated oven until custard is set. Remove and bring to room temperature. Chill overnight.
- Top with sugar and caramelize with a kitchen torch. If not, you can place ramekins under the broiler to caramelize sugar to serve.

Cheesecake

This is a New York-style cheesecake made with cream cheese and sour cream. Once it is in your repertoire, making it becomes second nature to you. The glaze can be chocolate ganache, blueberry, apricot, or raspberries depending on your choice

Crust:

1 recipe Graham cracker crust (page 38)

Filling:

2 (8 ounces) packages of cream cheese (room temperature)

3 large eggs

1 cup sugar

1-pint sour cream

1 lemon, zested

½ teaspoon vanilla extract

Topping:

1 cup apricot preserve

1 lemon, zested and juiced

2 tablespoons sugar

- Preheat the oven to 350° F.
- Line a springform pan with the graham cracker crust as in the suggested recipe, and set aside.
- Put room temperature cream cheese in the bowl of an electric mixer, and beat until smooth and free of lumps. Add eggs one at a time and beat slowly to well combine. Gradually add sugar and beat to a creamy consistency, about 2 minutes. Add sour cream, lemon zest, and vanilla. Continue to beat while scraping down the sides of the bowl, and the beaters a few times. The batter should be smooth but not overbeaten. Pour over the prepared graham cracker crust.
- Wrap the cheesecake pan in aluminum foil before putting it into a baking

pan. Transfer to the preheated oven and pour hot water into the pan until the water comes halfway up the sides of the cheesecake pan. Aluminum foil will keep the water from seeping into the cheesecake.

- Bake for 1 hour and 15 minutes. When done, the cheesecake should still jiggle because it needs to chill before it firms up. It is important not to overcook. Let it cool in the pan for 30 to 40 minutes. Cover it with plastic wrap and chill overnight.
- Run a knife around the pan to loosen the cake. Transfer to a cake pedestal or a plate and spread a thin layer of raspberry or apricot glaze topping over the surface.
- Glaze:
- Put apricot preserve in a small pan and cook over a gentle heat until it starts to bubble. Let it cool, then strain over the cheesecake. Refrigerate to let the topping set well before serving.
- To slice the cheesecakes, use a non-serrated knife, which is dipped in hot water. Wipe it clean and dip it in hot water after each cut.

Chocolate Cheesecake with Ganache

Crust:

1 recipe Graham cracker crust (page 38)

Filling:

2 (8 ounces) packages of cream cheese, at room temperature

1 cup granulated sugar

¼ cup cornstarch

1 teaspoon pure vanilla extract

½ teaspoon kosher salt

3 extra-large eggs, at room temperature

½ cup sour cream, at room temperature

5-ounce bittersweet chocolate, melted in a double boiler, and cooled

1 tablespoon instant espresso coffee

Ganache:

¼ pound semi-sweet chocolate

¼ cup heavy cream

- Preheat the oven to 350° F.
- Prepare springform pan by lining with a graham cracker crust.
- Beat the cream cheese, sugar, cornstarch, vanilla extract, and salt in a stand mixer until light and fluffy. Add eggs, one at a time, and continue to beat at medium speed scraping the sides as necessary. Add sour cream, melted and cooled chocolate, and 1-tablespoon expresso coffee and continue mixing at low speed. When thoroughly mixed, pour over the crust in a springform pan.
- Wrap the cheesecake pan in aluminum foil making sure to wrap the pan tightly and well to prevent water from seeping into the cake before you put it into a baking tray. Transfer to the preheated oven and pour hot water into the tray until the water comes halfway up the sides of the cheesecake pan. Bake for 1 hour and 15 minutes. When done, the cheesecake should still jiggle because it needs to chill before it firms

up. It is important not to overcook. Let it cool in the pan for 30 to 40 minutes. Cover it with plastic wrap and chill overnight.

- To make the ganache, bring the cream to a simmering boil. Meanwhile, put finely chopped chocolate in a heat-proof glass bowl. Pour hot cream over the chocolate and let it stand for 5 minutes. Stir well until all the chocolate is melted.
- Set it aside until the chocolate is cooled to room temperature. Remove the cake from the springform pan by carefully running a hot knife around the outside of the cake. Transfer it to a cake pedestal lined with pieces of parchment, and then drizzle the ganache over the top of the cheesecake. Smooth it with an offset spatula. Pull out the parchment pieces leaving the pedestal clean.
- Slice and serve.

Panna Cotta

Easy Italian custard. It is a very popular traditional dessert. When we went on a cruise around New Zealand and Australia, on board cruise ship we were frequently served delicious panna cotta with hot fudge topping for dinner dessert. Before that, I made it with honey, which is equally delicious.

2 cups heavy cream
1 cup milk
½ cup granulated sugar
1 packet unflavored gelatin
2 tablespoons cold water
2 teaspoons vanilla extract
1 cup hot fudge sauce (page 140)

- Place the cream, milk, and sugar in a saucepan and bring to a simmer while stirring until sugar is dissolved.
- Meanwhile, dissolve one packet of gelatin in 2 tablespoons of water and add to the simmering cream mixture. Stir and continue to heat until it steams (not boil) and gelatin is thoroughly dissolved. Add 1 teaspoon vanilla extract and mix to well combine.
- Divide the cream mixture equally into individual ramekins. Refrigerate overnight.
- To loosen the panna cotta from the ramekins, dip the bottom of each one into hot water for a few seconds.
- Slide a knife around the edge, and then carefully invert it over onto a serving plate.
- Drizzle 2 tablespoons of hot fudge on each serving.
- For variation, add grated chocolate, or mango pulp to the cream and milk mixture.

Dark Chocolate Cakes

These portion-sized chocolate cakes are moist and delicious. You can take the eating experience to another level by serving them with whipped cream and topped with dark chocolate sauce.

4 oz. dark chocolate
6 tablespoons unsalted butter
½ cup sugar
¼ cup all-purpose flour
3 eggs

- Preheat the oven to 350° F.
- In a saucepan, melt chocolate and butter over very low heat stirring.
- when chocolate is smooth, add sugar and stir to mix.
- Sieve flour into the mixture in small portions, stir to combine making sure that it does not burn. When all the ingredients are incorporated in a smooth sauce, pour equal amounts in 4 ramekins.
- Arrange the ramekins in a baking tray, and place them in the preheated oven. Add enough water to the tray until the water comes half the way up to the ramekins.
- Bake for 8 to 10 minutes.
- Serve immediately with whipped cream and chocolate sauce

Chocolate Mousse

½ pound chocolate
½ cup milk

- In a heat-proof glass bowl, microwave the chocolate for 30 seconds and then stir it. Place the bowl back in the microwave and repeat the process until the chocolate has melted completely.
- When the chocolate has melted, add the milk, stir and place the bowl into a bowl of ice cubes.
- Whisk vigorously until the mousse stiffens.
- Refrigerate for a few hours and serve with whipped cream topped with chocolate sauce.
- You can also serve with ice cream of your choice.

Chocolate sauce

4-ounce dark chocolate
3 tablespoons unsalted butter

- Melt the dark chocolate and butter in a saucepan over low heat until a smooth sauce forms. It is ready to serve.

Scandinavian Chocolate Gateau

½ pound dark chocolate
½ pound coconut fat, available in special stores (Trader Joe's carry small packets of coconut fat which are ideal.)
2 eggs
2 tablespoons granulated sugar
10 crackers, any kind as long as they are not too sweet
6 to 8 jelly beans (I used gumdrops)
1 cup orange marmalade
1 to 2 tablespoon instant coffee
8 to 10 raspberries

- Melt chocolate and coconut fat in a microwave until it is smooth.
- Meanwhile, beat 2 eggs and 2 tablespoon sugar until light and smooth.
- Add melted chocolate to the eggs slowly while whisking until it thickens.
- Pour 1/3 of the melted chocolate into a bread mold. Arrange one layer of crackers on top followed by spreading the marmalade generously. Pour another layer of chocolate on top.
- Add jelly beans, or gumdrops, and then a layer of crackers before pouring the final layer of chocolate.
- Refrigerate overnight. Remove from the refrigerator and put the mold in hot water to release the cake. Invert it on a plate.
- Sprinkle instant coffee generously and scatter raspberries on top and around to serve. Cut slices and serve with raspberries and ice cream.
- You can keep it frozen to consume later.

Quick Pastries and Cookies

» Bakers Tips:

The reasons why the muffins can go flat.

1. Over mixing the batter could be one of the reasons for the muffins to go flat. When the batter is overmixed, the gluten forms a tight network that prevents the gas bubbles from expanding.
2. If the batter is not mixed enough, gas bubbles are not created. And without the bubbles leavening does not work because leavening expands the gas bubbles which are created during mixing or creaming giving the muffins the needed rise.
3. If the amount of leavening agent is not enough, or the flour is wrong, there would be an insufficient rise in the dough.
4. Muffins won't rise If care is not taken when substituting baking powder with baking soda or vice versa. Because these two leavening agents have different functions. Baking soda works with doughs that are already acidic, whereas baking powder comes with cream of tartar, which is a built-in acidifier, and reacts with the batter which is not acidic.
5. Not resting the batter, or resting it too long can also affect the outcome. Resting time for single-acting and double-acting baking powder is different. If using single-acting baking powder, the muffins have to go in the oven right away, whereas with double-acting baking powder the dough needs to rest for 5-10 minutes to allow for the first action.
6. Sometimes it might be that the muffin cups are not filled enough to get enough rise. Since they don't double in size, they may look flatter if not filled almost to the edge of the cup.
7. Always use big blueberries, which are not overripe and cracked. And stems should be removed before use.

Blueberry Muffins

With this recipe, blueberry muffins are tender, moist, and filled with blueberries that burst in your mouth. It is an easy recipe that I had to tweak to get it right. I noted all the important points for this recipe to work. These points also apply when you use variations.

1¾ cup all-purpose flour
1 teaspoon baking powder
¼ teaspoon baking soda
½ teaspoon salt
1 cup granulated sugar
7 tablespoons vegetable oil
¼ cup buttermilk
¼ cup sour cream
2 large eggs
1½ cups blueberries
1 tablespoon raw sugar
Crumb Topping
⅓ cup flour
1 ½ tablespoon granulated sugar
3 tablespoons salted butter, cold and cut in small dice

- Add 1/3 cup flour, 1 ½ tablespoons sugar, and diced butter to a food processor and pulse until the mixture resembles crumbs, and fluffy not too sandy. Set aside.
- For Blueberry Muffins
- Preheat oven to 400°F.
- Stir together flour, baking powder, baking soda, and salt in a bowl until well combined, about 30 seconds.
- In another mixing bowl, whisk granulated sugar, oil, buttermilk, sour cream, and eggs until fully blended.

- Add flour mix to the bowl and fold with a rubber spatula until well blended. The key is not to over blend but stop when slightly lumpy for fluffy muffins.
- Gently fold in blueberries to prevent bleeding. Divide mixture evenly among 12 paper-lined muffin cups.
- Fluff prepared crumb topping with a fork and evenly sprinkle on each muffin. Follow it with sprinkling raw sugar on top.
- Bake in a preheated oven for 18-22 minutes or until golden brown and toothpick inserted in the center comes out clean.
- Let them cool slightly in a muffin pan before serving.
- This has been a foolproof recipe that we enjoy tremendously. Please try it.

Chocolate Cupcakes

Cupcakes are not only easy to make, but they are also easy to eat and enjoy.

12 tablespoons room temperature butter
2/3 cup granulated sugar
2/3 cup brown sugar
2 large eggs
2 teaspoons vanilla
1 cup room temperature buttermilk
½ cup sour cream
2 tablespoons freshly brewed coffee
1 1/3 cup all-purpose flour
1 cup unsweetened cocoa powder
½ teaspoon kosher salt
1 ½ teaspoon baking soda

- Beat room temperature butter, granulated sugar, and brown sugar in a standup mixer until thoroughly mixed.
- Prepare 2 muffin trays each with 12 cups by lining with paper liners and set aside.
- Break eggs in a bowl to prevent stray shells in the mixture. Add eggs to the butter-sugar mixture slowly to allow it to get well combined. Also, add vanilla while mixing.
- In a bowl, mix room temperature buttermilk, sour cream, and 2 tablespoons freshly brewed coffee
- Sift flour, cocoa, salt, and soda in one bowl.
- Add 1/3 portion of each dry and wet ingredient alternatively to the butter and egg mixture until all the ingredients are combined into a smooth batter.
- Using an ice cream scoop fill each cup of prepared muffin cups with an

equal amount of cupcake batter.

- Bake in a preheated 350° F. oven for 30 to 35 minutes. Remove from the oven and let them cool to room temperature.

Cream puffs

Pate choux batter recipe (page 35)

Line a baking sheet with parchment paper and set it aside.

When pâté choux batter is ready, drop the batter with a mini ice cream scoop or pipe the dough into a desired shape 3 in. apart onto a parchment-lined baking sheet.

Use egg wash to brush over puffs.

Bake at 375° F. preheated oven for about 25 minutes or golden brown. Transfer to a wire rack after cutting a slit into each to let the steam escape. Let them cool

Dust with powdered sugar.

Cut cream puffs in half and fill with freshly whipped cream (page 139).

Eclairs

- To make an éclair, line a baking tray with parchment paper after drawing lines 3-in. long and 1 ½ inch apart. Turn it upside down ready to pipe the dough onto it.
- Use a pastry bag with a tip which measures ½ in. and fill the bag with the choux batter.
- Pipe a little of the batter in each corner of the tray under the parchment to glue it in place and to ensure that the parchment does not move.
- Pipe the batter along the lines and smooth out any uneven surface by leveling the dough with a wet finger.
- Bake at 400°F. preheated oven for 30 minutes or golden brown. Transfer to a wire rack after cutting a slit into each to let the steam escape. Let them cool.
- Make a hole on both ends of each éclair and fill with whipped cream (page 139). When you fill from one end it should squeeze out from the other side if properly filled. Dip in the chocolate glaze on one side

Orange-Currant Scones

3 cups all-purpose flour
½ -cup sugar
1/8-teaspoon salt
4 teaspoons baking powder
½ pound (2 stick) butter, cut into small cubes, refrigerated
½ cup raisins
1 tablespoon orange zest, freshly grated
1 large egg
½ cup whole milk

- Preheat the oven to 375°F. Line a baking sheet with parchment paper.
- In a large bowl, whisk together flour, sugar, salt, and baking powder until well combined.
- Add butter cubes, and with your fingertips rub it into the flour until the butter is the size of peas.
- Add raisins and zest and toss to mix evenly.
- Whisk the egg, and milk before adding to the dry Ingredients.
- Make a well in the center of the flour, add egg and milk mixture and bring the flour together to form a ball gathering it from all around.
- Knead just to make a smooth ball of dough. Make a disc and roll like a wheel to smooth out edges.
- Roll out the dough disc to one-inch thickness, and cut into wedges.
- Place on the parchment-lined baking sheet, brush with milk, and bake for about 30 minutes. These are best served warm from the oven.

Buttermilk Biscuits

4 cups self-rising flour
½ cup (1 stick) cold butter
1 1/3 cup cold buttermilk
All-purpose flour for dusting the work surface

- Preheat the oven to 425° F.
- Cut half the butter in thin slices and the other half in cubes.
- Add self-rising flour to a large bowl. Add the butter and cut into the flour with a pastry blender until some butter is in pea-sized pieces.
- Add very cold buttermilk, saving some of it, and mix. If you need more, you can add the remaining buttermilk and mix—transfer onto a well-floured work surface. Knead, while bringing all the loose flour making sure to smooth out the crumbling edges by incorporating them into the dough. Flatten the dough down until it is 2-inches thick. And then flour a 2 ½ -inch biscuit cutter to cut straight down into the dough. Don't turn or spin the biscuit cutter because that would stop the edges from rising. Arrange on a lightly oiled cast-iron skillet.
- Assemble all the scraps and cut biscuits until all the dough is used up. You will get about 14 biscuits. You may have to bake in two batches.
- Brush the biscuits with melted salted butter and bake for about 30 minutes or until golden brown (depending on your oven, it may take longer).
- Transfer to a wire rack and let them cool slightly before serving

Banana Bread

This recipe of banana bread is foolproof. The texture and color depend on the ripeness and quantity of bananas. 4 or 5 small and very ripe bananas result in a soft texture and dark brown color. If you want firmer texture and lighter color use 2 or 3 less ripened bananas. Make the one you find more to your liking.

1¾ cups all-purpose flour
1¼ teaspoon baking powder
½ teaspoon baking soda
½ teaspoon salt
2/3-cup sugar
1/3 cup shortening
2 eggs
2 tablespoons milk
4-5 small, very ripe bananas (1 cup), mashed
¼ cup chopped walnuts or nuts on hand

- Preheat oven to 350°F.
- In a large bowl, well whisk flour, baking powder, baking soda, and salt.
- In another bowl cream sugar and shortening with an electric beater, or by hand, until smooth.
- Add 1 egg at a time and beat until smooth. Add milk and mix well.
- Add half of the flour and mashed banana and continue to mix well before adding the rest of the flour and banana and continue to mix.
- When all the ingredients are well combined, add chopped walnuts and fold to spread the nuts evenly throughout the mixture.
- Grease, and flour a bread mold, and transfer the batter to it.
- Bake in a preheated oven for 55 minutes or until an inserted knife comes out clean.
- When the bread is baked, remove it from the oven and cool it on a wire

rack. When the bread is at the room temperature, run a knife around it and invert on a cutting board and flip-up to the right side. Slice and serve.

Biscotti

Biscotti is a great breakfast treat, or it can be a delicious snack. Easy to make and easy to store for at least 2 weeks in a cookie jar. I always make it for my family and they enjoy the crisp treats every time.

2 cups all-purpose flour
1 teaspoons baking powder
¼ teaspoon salt
1 cup plus 1 tablespoon granulated sugar
2 large eggs, beaten with pinch salt
3 tablespoons unsalted butter, melted and cooled
1 teaspoon vanilla
½ cup walnuts, or ½ cup whole almonds, slightly roasted
½ cup almonds roughly chopped (if using almonds)
¼ cup plump golden raisins(optional)

- Preheat the oven to 375°F.
- Grease a baking sheet, and line it with parchment paper, and lightly grease the paper too. Set it aside.
- In a large bowl, add flour, baking powder, and salt and mix well.
- In another bowl, cream butter and sugar until smooth.
- Add one egg at a time and beat until smooth before adding the next one. When the mixture is pale in color and has a smooth finish, add vanilla and mix well.
- Add dry ingredients mix to the egg mixture and stir to form a dough.
- Add nuts of your choice along with golden raisins if using and mix well.
- Pat the dough into a disc, cover with plastic and refrigerate for 30 minutes. Chilling it helps to get it firm and easy to handle.
- Transfer to a work surface and divide the batter in half.
- Form each half into a 2x7 inch loaf and place on a greased baking trays making sure to space them out to allow room to spread.

- Brush the top lightly with some oil.
- Lower the temperature of the oven to 350°F, and bake the loaves for 25 to 30 minutes, rotating the sheet halfway through baking.
- Remove from the oven and let the loaves cool.
- Transfer loaves to a cutting board. With a serrated knife, slice each loaf into 1-inch-thick slices on a slight bias.
- Arrange the slices with one cut side up on a cookie sheet and bake for 10 minutes. Flip slices and bake for another 20 minutes or until golden brown.
- Remove from the oven, and let it cool on a rack completely before serving.

French Palmier

This recipe makes cookies with puff pastry. It goes by different names such as elephant ears, fan biscuits, or French palmier. To make the cookies, cinnamon Sugar is sprinkled on the bottom and top of the puff pastry sheet before rolling to a 13-inch square. It is folded as if closing a book. Cut into 1-inch-thick cookies and baked in 425°F. oven for 6 to 8 minutes.

½ cup sugar, divided
Pinch salt
¼ teaspoon cinnamon
store-bought puff pastry comes with two sheets

- Preheat the oven to 425°F. Arrange a shelf in the center of the oven to prevent the bottom of the cookies from burning.
- In a bowl mix ¼ cup sugar and salt. Divide the mixture into 4 equal parts. Sprinkle ¼ of the sugar mixture evenly on a work surface.
- Place 1 sheet of defrosted pastry flat onto the sugar mixture. sprinkle the other ¼ of sugar and cinnamon mixture on top of the pastry.
- Roll the pastry pressing the sugar mixture into the top and bottom of the pastry, and until the pastry is a 13-inch square.
- Fold the sides of the pastry to the 1/3-division lines, and fold the sides again bringing them to the center. Now fold the sides as if closing a book. It will form six layers.
- Cut it into 1-inch slices. Line a baking sheet with parchment paper and arrange the palmier on it.
- Bake the cookies for 6 to 8 minutes on one side until caramelized at the bottom, then turn them over and bake for another 5 minutes to caramelize on the other side.
- Transfer to a rack to cool before serving.
- Let the baking sheet cool by running cold water on it, and repeat the process to make palmier with the second sheet.

Pancakes

Pancakes make a great weekend breakfast. Mix wet and dry ingredients separately and combine just before cooking. Don't over mix. The slightly lumpy batter will give you fluffy pancakes.

1 cup all-purpose flour
1 tablespoon white sugar
1 teaspoon baking powder
¼ teaspoon baking soda
¼ teaspoon salt
1 cup buttermilk,
1½ tablespoon unsalted butter, melted and cooled
1 medium egg, beaten

- Mix flour, sugar, baking powder, baking soda, and salt in a large bowl.
- Whisk buttermilk, melted butter, and one medium egg in a bowl.
- Make a well in the dry ingredients and pour the wet ingredients.
- Mix until just incorporated with a few lumps. It is important not to overmix.
- Heat a griddle over medium-high heat, don't overheat. Lightly oil it. Too much oil will make the pancakes taste greasy.
- Pour ¼ cup batter with a measuring cup on the griddle, in a steady stream in the center, for each pancake.
- Cook until brown on one side, and bubbly on top before flipping to cook the other side until brown. About one or two minutes on each side.
- Serve hot with maple syrup.

Brownies

Brownies are a popular item with young and old alike. There are a lot of versions and mostly quite easy. Some are cakey and others are fudgy. It is vital not to beat much after adding eggs to prevent the meringue-like crust.

2 ounces unsweetened chocolate
1/3 cup Crisco
2 large eggs
2/3 cup flour
1 teaspoon vanilla
½ teaspoon salt
½ teaspoon baking powder
1 cup chopped pecans

- Place the rack in the center of the oven.
- Preheat the oven to 350°F.
- Melt chocolate and Crisco in the microwave until smooth.
- Beat eggs until light in color, about 2 minutes. Add melted and cooled chocolate and stir to mix thoroughly. Add flour, vanilla, salt, and baking powder and mix well.
- Fold in pecans reserving some of them for garnish.
- Transfer the batter to a cake pan and garnish with reserved pecans. Bake for 25 minutes or until a toothpick inserted in the center comes out clean.
- If you beat the eggs too long top may crack, but the interior will be moist. Cut into 2-inch squares. Top with warm caramel sauce, and a small scoop of ice cream to serve.

Black and White Shortbread Cookies

¾ pound (3 sticks) unsalted butter, room temperature
1 cup granulated sugar
1 teaspoon vanilla extract
3 ½ cups all-purpose flour
¼ teaspoon kosher salt
½ -cup grated semisweet chocolate

- Preheat the oven to 350°F.
- Line a cookie sheet with parchment paper and set it aside ready for baking the cookies
- In the bowl of a stand mixer, put butter, sugar, vanilla, flour, and salt.
- Beat the mixture with a paddle attachment until it comes together in a dough.
- Transfer the dough to the work surface and bring it together in a ball and then pat it down to a disc. Wrap the disc in plastic wrap and chill it for 30 minutes or more. When ready to roll, remove it from the refrigerator and let it soften enough to roll it with ease.
- Always roll from the center to the edge turning 45° before each roll to get an even finish. If it sticks, sprinkle a little flour under it. Roll until ½-inch thick. Use a finger cookie cutter or 3 ½ inches round cookie cutter to cut out the cookies.
- Arrange the cookies on the prepared cookie sheet and bake for 20 minutes or until golden brown.
- Transfer cookie to a rack to cool. Meanwhile, put ½ cup grated semisweet chocolate in a microwave-safe bowl. Microwave for 30 seconds. Stir, and 30 seconds more until chocolate is melted and is smooth.
- Take one cookie at a time in your left hand and use a spoon to pour some melted chocolate at the bottom half and return it to the rack to set.
- Enjoy when set.

Madeleines (French Butter Cakes)

Madeleines are French butter cakes and are generally considered cookies. These sponge cakes need baking pans with special shell-shaped molds. These tea-time treats can only be made if you have the required equipment.

8 tablespoons unsalted butter, well softened
¼ cup granulated sugar
2 eggs, beaten until light and fluffy
1 teaspoon vanilla extract
½ cup all-purpose flour
pinch salt
½ teaspoon ground cinnamon

- Preheat oven to 375°F. Butter and flour 12 (3 inches) madeleine molds and set aside.
- In a bowl of a stand mixer with a paddle attachment, cream butter, and sugar. Add eggs 1 at a time and beat for 5 minutes. While beating add vanilla and salt.
- Sift flour and add to the egg mixture in three addition folding after each addition until smooth and well mixed.
- Spoon batter into madeleine mold until well filled.
- Bake in a pre-heated oven for 20 minutes or until golden brown.
- Tops should spring back when gently pressed with your fingertips.
- Remove from the oven and cool slightly, before transferring to a rack. Sprinkle granulated sugar, and eat while they are still warm. eaten right away is the best way to enjoy madeleine.

Macarons

These hard to make dainty little cookies are very popular even among fussy kids. With very few ingredients, these cookies are delicious, light, crispy outside and chewy inside. Almond powder and egg white contribute to their melt in your mouth quality. Recipe requires older, room temperature egg whites for its stiff meringue. Almond powder needs to be extra fine and smooth for a perfectly smooth finish to the cookie. Measuring and sifting through a fine mesh sieve without pressing at the end is important. You can discard the last few particles.

1 cup powdered sugar
2/3 cup almond powder
2 large egg whites, room temperature
¼ teaspoon salt
¼ cup superfine sugar
2 to 3 drops desired food color, gel color
Filling:
¼ cup butter cream, jam, ganache, or any desired filling ,your preference.

- preheat oven to 300°F.
- Line 2 baking trays with parchment paper and set aside.
- Measure confectioner sugar and almond powder in a bowl by spooning into a measuring cup and leveling off with a knife. Whisk to combine.
- Using fine mesh sieve, sift confectioner sugar and almond powder and discard impurities. Whiz the dry ingredients in a food processor and sieve again. Repeat the process one more time to get very refined dry ingredients.
- In a stand mixer beat egg whites and salt until frothy. Start adding sugar and continue to beat until the meringue reaches soft peak stage. Add desired gel food color at this point. Continue to beat until meringue reaches stiff peak stage.

- Transfer the stiff meringue on top of the dry ingredients. Start folding carefully to prevent deflating the egg whites. Folding is done by cutting the mixture vertically through, bringing the spatula across the bottom of the bowl and up the nearest side pressing gently. Fold until thoroughly incorporated. Do it by turning the bowl and scraping down the bowl until mixture is free of lumps. You will know that it is ready when it drizzles to form thin ribbons which do not break when you make a figure 8 with it.
- Fit the pastry bag with round, #12 tip and fill the bag with the prepared batter.
- Use some of the batter under each corner of the parchment paper to keep it in place in the baking tray. Start piping uniform 1 ¼ inch circles on the prepared baking tray, 12 on each tray. Firmly tap the tray on the work surface to remove any bubbles. Let the cookies stand at room temperature for 2 hours or more for the shells to dry out.
- Bake on a double baking tray to prevent burning. Bake for in a 300°F oven for 15 to 17 minutes turning half way through for even cooking. Bake one tray at a time and remove to a rack to cool completely.
- Pipe filling onto the back of half the shells and use the other half to make a sandwiches.
- They are best consumed within 24 hours at room temperature. Can be refrigerated for 2 to 3 days in an air tight container. Can be frozen for longer, but better to freeze the shells without filling in an air tight container. When ready to use, remove from the freezer ahead of time and then assemble with desired filling to serve.

Chocolate Chip Cookies

2 ½ cups all-purpose flour
1 teaspoon baking soda
½ teaspoon salt
1 cup (2-sticks) butter, softened
¾ cup granulated sugar
¾ cup brown sugar
1 teaspoon vanilla extract
2 large eggs
2 cups (12-ounces) semi-sweet chocolate morsels
1 cup chopped walnuts

- Preheat oven to 375° F.
- Combine flour, baking soda, and salt in a bowl.
- Beat softened butter, granulated sugar, brown sugar, in a stand mixer with a paddle attachment or by hand in a large bowl until it is creamy, and add vanilla and mix.
- Add eggs, one at a time, beating after each addition, and then add flour mixture while still beating on medium speed until well incorporated.
- Fold in chocolate morsels, and chopped walnuts into the batter.
- Use a medium-sized ice cream scoop to drop the batter on parchment paper-lined baking sheets.
- Bake for 9 to 12 minutes or until golden brown.
- At first cool on the baking sheet for a few minutes.
- Transfer to a wire rack to cool completely on all sides.

Sugar Cookies

Sugar cookies have been a global favorite for time immemorial. Their popularity is due to their delicious taste and ease of making. They are my grandchildren's and all kids' go-to cookies.

2 stick (1cup) unsalted butter, softened
1 ½ cup sugar
1 large egg
1 teaspoon vanilla
2 ¾ cups all-purpose flour
½ teaspoon baking powder
1 teaspoon baking soda
additional sugar

- preheat oven to 375° F.
- In a bowl of a stand mixer, cream butter and sugar until fluffy. Add egg and vanilla and combine.
- whisk flour, baking powder, and baking soda in another bowl until well incorporated. Gradually add the flour to creamed butter mixture and mix until it comes together. Transfer to the work surface and break off enough dough to roll into 1 inch balls. Continue to do it until all the dough is used up, about 48 balls.
- Roll each ball in additional sugar and place on an ungreased baking sheet giving them room because they spread.
- Since it is enough for 48 cookies, you would need 2 baking sheets to bake two batches of cookies.
- Bake in a preheated oven for 10 to 12 minutes until light brown. Remove from the oven and transfer to a wire rack to cool.

Greek Cookies

3 sticks (1 ½ cups) unsalted butter
½ teaspoon salt
1 egg yolk
¼ cup powdered sugar
1-teaspoon vanilla
2-tablespoon brandy
3 cups all-purpose flour
¼ cup powdered sugar for dredging the cookies

- Preheat oven to 350° F.
- Beat butter with ½ teaspoon salt in a bowl until it is fluffy and is lighter yellow.
- Add egg yolk and beat to mix well.
- Add powdered sugar, vanilla, and brandy and combine to mix well.
- Add flour and fold with a spatula until it is smooth.
- Transfer to a working surface and pull in all the loose bits of flour and flatten to a rectangle. Wrap in plastic to refrigerate for 30 minutes.
- Remove from the refrigerator, unwrap and cut into 4 to 5 sections. Break off small balls of dough and shape them into moon-shaped, discs or desired shapes.
- Place on a greased cookie sheet and bake in a 350° F oven for 30 minutes or until golden brown.
- Transfer to a cooling rack.
- Spread powdered sugar on a platter and dredge cookies into the sugar before storing in an airtight jar.

Heart Cookies

2½ sticks (10 oz.) butter
¾ cup granulated sugar
2 1/3 cups all-purpose flour, plus additional flour for rolling the cookies
½ cup ground almonds
½ teaspoon ground cinnamon
¼ teaspoon ground nutmeg
1 cup seedless raspberry jam
Equipment needed:
1 heart-shaped cookie cutter
1 small star-shaped cookie cutter

- Preheat oven to 350° F.
- In a bowl, whip butter in a stand mixer.
- Add sugar and continue mixing until light and fluffy, about 5 minutes.
- In another bowl combine flour, ground almonds, cinnamon, and nutmeg.
- Add flour mixture to the butter cleaning the sides with a rubber spatula. Blend until all the flour comes together.
- Remove onto a work surface and form into a ball pulling all the loose flour together.
- Divide the dough into two parts and wrap each part in a piece of plastic wrap. Put in the refrigerator for 15 minutes or more before rolling for cookies.
- When ready take one piece at a time, and roll to 1/8-inch thickness. Cut cookies with a heart-shaped cutter. Arrange on a cookie sheet and bake for 12 to 15 minutes.
- While the first batch is in the oven, remove the rest of the dough from the fridge and roll to 1/8-inch thickness.
- Cut using the heart-shaped cutter, but this time use a star-shaped cutter to cut in the center of each one and arrange on a baking sheet.
- When the first batch is done, let them cool and bake the second for about

the same time as the first.

- When all the cookies are done and cooled, spread about ¼ teaspoon of jam on the hearts and top each one with the star-centered one.
- Dust with powdered sugar if so desired.

Chocolate Whoopie Pies

Whoopie pies are a lot easier to make than they look. A great treat for kids lunch boxes, snacks or tea time treat for adults.

1 stick unsalted butter, softened
1 cup granulated sugar
1 teaspoon vanilla extract
1 1/3 cups all-purpose flour
¾ cup cocoa powder
1 ½ teaspoon baking soda
½ teaspoon baking powder
½ teaspoon salt
1 cup buttermilk, room temperature
1 large egg

- Butter cream with corn syrup recipe (page 141)
- Preheat the oven to 400 degree F and line 2 baking sheets with parchment paper and set aside. Adjust the oven rack to the middle position.
- In a bowl of a stand mixer with the paddle attachment, cream butter, and sugar until fluffy and well combined. Add vanilla extract and continue creaming for 1 to 2 minutes.
- Meanwhile, stir together all-purpose flour, cocoa powder, baking soda, baking powder, and salt and set aside.
- Add buttermilk and 1 large egg to the butter mixture and mix until well combined. Add dry ingredient slowly and combine thoroughly until smooth batter forms.
- Use a mini ice cream scoop to put the batter on prepared baking sheets until all the dough is used up. 2 to three batches of cookies will fit onto each sheet. This batter will be enough for 16 to 18 pies.
- Bake each batch for 12 minutes. Bring to room temperature.
- Put one tablespoon buttercream on the flat surface of one cookie and

sandwich with the flat side of the other one. Press gently to spread the buttercream to the edges. Serve.

Chocolate Truffles Cookies

4 ounces bittersweet chocolate
4 ounces semi-sweet chocolate
1 stick unsalted butter
4 cups powdered sugar
2 tablespoons rum (optional)
Chocolate sprinkles

- Grate all 8 ounces of chocolate and melt stirring on a double boiler. While melting cut up one stick of butter and add to the melting chocolate.
- Remove from the heat and add rum. Mix to combine.
- Add 4 cups powdered sugar and mix with hands.
- When all the sugar and chocolate come together put in the refrigerator for 10 to 15 minutes.
- Remove from the refrigerator and make balls about 1 ½ inch diameter. Roll the balls into chocolate sprinkles, pressing hard enough to get some of the sprinkles into the balls.
- There is no cooking involved, and the cookies can be stored in the refrigerated

Serving Sauces and Toppings for Desserts

Salted Caramel

1 cup sugar
¼ cup water
¾ cup heavy cream
3½ tablespoon unsalted butter
1 teaspoon vanilla
1 teaspoon kosher salt

- Combine sugar and water in a heavy-bottomed saucepan.
- Cook on medium-low heat until sugar dissolves.
- Once the sugar is dissolved, increase heat and bring the mixture to a boil without stirring.
- With a wet pastry brush, brush the sides of the pan to prevent crystal formation.
- Continue cooking on high heat until the syrup is a deep amber color.
- Remove from heat and whisk in heavy cream, being careful of the steam release.
- Add butter, vanilla, and salt and stir to combine.
- Transfer to a jar or desired container and let it cool.
- Caramel can keep for 2 weeks in the refrigerator.
- Reheat in the microwave before serving.

Whipped Cream

1 cup heavy cream
pinch cream of tartar
2 tablespoons sugar

- Keep a metal bowl and metal whisk in the freezer for 30 minutes. Also, place the cream in the freezer for 5 minutes to chill.
- Pour cream, into the bowl of standup mixer and beat to soft peaks.
- Meanwhile, mix the sugar and cream of tartar. While the mixer is running, add the sugar in a slow stream and beat until stiff peaks form.
- Serve with the pavlova or any desserts you wish.

Hot fudge Sauce

1 ½ cup sugar
1 cup unsweetened cocoa powder
1 cup heavy cream, or whole milk
½ cup (1 stick) butter
1 teaspoon vanilla extract
pinch salt

- In a heavy saucepan, whisk sugar, cocoa powder, and milk until well blended and smooth
- Bring to a simmering boil while stirring continuously. Add butter and continue to cook stirring until it thickens.
- Remove from heat and stir in vanilla extract and salt. Let it cool before serving on panna cotta, ice cream, or other desserts of your choice.

Buttercream with Corn Syrup

Easy, delicious, and wonderful frosting by any standard.

½ cup (1 stick) softened unsalted butter
2 tablespoons light corn syrup
1 teaspoon vanilla
Pinch salt
4 cups confectioner sugar
2 tablespoons milk
food coloring as desired

- In a standing mixer with a paddle attachment, beat butter, corn syrup, vanilla, and salt until light and fluffy.
- Sift powdered sugar with a medium-mesh strainer to remove all the lumps and add it with milk to the bowl and beat at low speed while scraping down the sides. Adjust consistency to a desired spreading level by adding a little milk or sugar.
- Add coloring as desired.
- It can be stored in an airtight container until ready to use. Whip with a hand beater or in a mixer before use.

Pastry Cream

1 ¼ cups milk
¼ cup granulated sugar
½ teaspoon vanilla extract
3 large egg yolks
3 tablespoons all-purpose flour, or cornstarch
2 tablespoons unsalted butter
Pinch salt

- To a saucepan add milk, and heat over medium heat.
- In a large bowl, combine the egg yolks, and sugar and whisk until it is lighter in color.
- Sift flour, or corn starch, and salt together and mix to combine. Add to the egg mixture, mixing until you get a smooth paste
- When the milk comes to a boil, remove it from the heat and add vanilla extract.
- Start adding milk slowly to the yolk mixture while stirring continuously to prevent eggs from scrambling.
- When half the milk is added, transfer all the yolk mixture to the milk saucepan over medium heat.
- Continue heating while whisking making sure to scrape all sides of the saucepan until the mixture comes to a boil.
- Let it boil for 1 minute, still stirring constantly until it becomes thick.
- Remove from heat and add butter and salt. Cook for another 60 seconds. Strain to remove any solid bits it may have and the resulting cream is extra smooth.
- Cover the cream by putting plastic wrap directly on it to prevent any skin from forming on top of the cream.
- Chill and serve.

Indian Desserts

Coconut Burfi

2 cups fresh coconut grated or grated sweetened coconut
1 cup sugar
½ cup heavy cream
Pinch cardamom powder
1 teaspoon orange color
¼ cup powdered sugar
½ tablespoon ghee, oil, or butter for greasing the dish

- Grease an 8x8 dish to use later.
- Heat a non-stick pan on medium heat. Add grated coconut, sugar, heavy cream, cardamom powder, and enough orange food color (about 1 teaspoon or a little more to get good orange color) and cook stirring for 12 minutes or until all the extra moisture evaporates.
- Remove the pan from heat and add powdered sugar and stir to combine well.
- Transfer the coconut mixture to the prepared dish and spread the mixture evenly.
- Let it cool and then cut into squares, and serve. You can store it in an airtight container in the refrigerator for about a week.

Sugar Syrup Soft Ball Stage:

For Double ka meetha (Indian Breading Pudding), 2 different types of sugar syrup are used. The beginning part of the recipe calls for simple syrup. In the end, I decided to use the softball stage technique to make caramel bits to garnish the desserts. This gives the dessert a delicious crunch and sweetness which is unforgettable.

To make the caramel bits, heat the sugar and water until the syrup registers 234°F-245°F. At this point, drop the syrup into ice water. Then gather it into a ball. This should be pliable enough to be flattened and cut into small bits ready to be sprinkled as a garnish over the dessert.

Double Ka Meetha (Indian Bread Pudding)

10 white bread slices
1 cup ghee or Crisco
2 cups sugar
1 cup water
½ teaspoon cardamom powder, finely ground
2 cups milk
1 cup heavy cream
1-cup condensed milk
8-ounce ricotta cheese
heavy pinch saffron
½ cup slivered almonds
Garnish:
1 cup sugar
¼ cup water to make softball caramel (Technique page 145)

- Preheat oven 350° F.
- Remove the crust from the bread slices and toast in a toaster. and then fry with a little ghee or Crisco in a skillet turning to make sure that browning is even on both sides- It should be darker brown.
- In a saucepan mix sugar and water and cook until sugar dissolves. Continue to simmer to get slightly thickened simple syrup. Add finely ground cardamom powder and mix.
- In another heavy saucepan mix milk, heavy cream, and condensed milk and heat until scalded (bring it up to a slow simmer). Whip ricotta cheese in a bowl until well blended and add along with saffron strands to the hot milk. Make sure to blend well.
- Arrange toasted bread slices in a deep baking tray. Pour the sugar syrup over it. Let the bread soak in the syrup for about 20 minutes.

- And then pour ricotta milk over it, and seal it with aluminum foil.
- Bake in the preheated oven for 1 hour, or until the milk is absorbed.
- Remove from oven and let it rest covered and bring it to room temperature.
- Transfer to a serving dish, garnish with slivered almonds and scatter bits of soft caramel on top to serve.

Vermicelli Dessert

The first time I ate vermicelli dessert was in one of the restaurants in Cairo, Egypt where we were staying because it was one of the stops on our way to India. We were in the dining room for breaking our Ramadan fast. They had a dessert table all along the wall in a huge dining area. The vermicelli was one of the amazing slew of desserts they had. I can easily say that it was the best dessert I have ever eaten in my life. This attempt at trying to replicate it, I think, comes very close.

½ pack vermicelli (250 grams)
1 cup sugar
1 cup water
2 tablespoon ghee, or unsalted butter
1 tablespoon oil
Dry fruits, and nuts-almond, pistachios, and 2 tablespoons chironji (charoli)- soaked in hot water and then peeled.
1 tablespoon raisins
1 tablespoon milk
½ teaspoon cardamom powder
¼ cup milk

- Gently crush vermicelli into 2-3-inch-long pieces with your hands while still in the packaging.
- Mix sugar and water in a saucepan and bring to a simmer and let it simmer until all the sugar is dissolved and simple syrup is ready. Set it aside.
- In a heavy, wide saucepan, heat ghee, or butter and oil together on medium-low heat (mixing oil and butter prevents the butter from burning).
- When butter is melted, lower heat further, and fry fruits and nuts together very lightly and briefly, and transfer to a platter. Set aside.
- Meanwhile, soak raisins in 1 tablespoon of milk.

- Add crushed vermicelli to the same saucepan and fry stirring until light brown. Stay with it because there is a very thin line between light brown and charred.
- Add cardamom powder to ¼ cup milk and mix well. Add it to vermicelli and cook stirring to soften about 1 to 2 minutes.
- Add soaked raisins along with the prepared syrup to the vermicelli and stir evenly to soak vermicelli in the syrup. Cook stirring for about 3 minutes and remove from heat. Transfer to a decorative platter. It will still cook in its own heat.
- Sprinkle fried nuts and dried fruits on top.
- Let it cool to room temperature.
- And then further chill in the refrigerator to serve.

Kaddu ka Halwa (Bottle Gourd Dessert)

Kaddu ka halwa is a popular dessert all over India. Bottle gourd is peeled and a soft, seedy center is discarded. The firm parts are finely grated to make the dessert.

1 medium-size bottle gourd (kaddu), peeled, and the soft, seedy center discarded. Finely grate the remaining firm parts
2 tablespoons butter or ghee
¼ cup mixture of peeled and thinly sliced pistachios, and almonds.
1 tablespoon raisin soaked in 1 tablespoon milk
1½ cup milk
1½ cup sugar
½ teaspoon cardamom powder
4 or 5 almonds, peeled and thinly sliced, lightly roasted for garnish

- In a heavy-bottomed skillet, heat ghee or butter until it melts.
- Add nuts and lightly fry them, and transfer to a platter to be added later.
- Meanwhile, soak raisins in one tablespoon of milk and set aside.
- Add grated kaddu (bottle gourd) and continue frying until all its moisture is absorbed about 15 to 20 minutes.
- Add milk, and sugar and cook on low heat until kaddu (bottle gourd) is tender.
- Add fried nuts, raisins with the milk, and cardamom powder, and continue to stir fry until the oil separates on the sides.
- Serve in a bowl and garnish with thinly sliced almonds.

Kheer Recipe

Kheer is also called Fereni and is a traditional dessert in Indian or Iranian cuisine. Simply said, it is a slightly thinner version of rice pudding which is flavored with cardamoms, raisins, saffron, and other desired nuts.

3½ cups milk
1/3 cup ground rice
3 tablespoons tapioca (sabudana) soaked for 15 to 20 minutes
1 cup sugar
¼ teaspoon ground cardamom
1 tablespoon raisins

For Garnish:

2 tablespoons mixture of sliced almonds and pistachios

- In a bowl, soak the ground rice in enough milk and set aside.
- Add milk to a large heavy saucepan and heat until it comes to a boil.
- Lower heat immediately, and let it simmer to reduce by ¾ of the original amount.
- Add tapioca(sabudana) and cook until translucent, then add sugar stirring to dissolve it completely.
- Once the sugar is completely dissolved, stir the soaked rice well to make a smooth mixture, and add in a slow stream to the hot milk while whisking to avoid lumps from forming.
- Add ground cardamoms and raisins. Cook stirring continuously on very low heat to prevent sticking to the bottom and burning.
- Once it reaches a creamy, thick desired consistency, remove it from the heat and allow the kheer to cool thoroughly.
- Garnish with prepared nut and serve.

Semolina Coconut Cake (Basbousa)

Basbousa is a traditional Middle Eastern Cake. It is made by cooking semolina, and coconut in a simple syrup. It is usually flavored with cardamom and rose water, but you can use other flavorings of your choice.

1 ¼ cup whole milk
heavy pinch saffron
1 ½ cup semolina
2 cups desiccated coconut
1 teaspoon baking powder
½ teaspoon baking soda
½ teaspoon salt
½ cup sugar
1 cup melted, unsalted butter
2 large eggs
1 cup yogurt

syrup:

1 cup water
2 cups sugar
½ teaspoon cardamom powder
juice of 1 lemon (2 tablespoons)
1 tablespoon rose water(optional)

Garnish:

¼ cup pistachios

- In a heavy milk saucepan, scald (when you see bubbles along the edges, the milk is scalded) 1¼ cup milk with a generous pinch of saffron.
- Meanwhile, whisk semolina, desiccated coconut, baking powder, baking soda, and ½ teaspoon salt, and set it aside.
- In a stand mixer bowl, cream ½ cup sugar and 1 cup melted, unsalted

butter, until it is light and fluffy. Add eggs and mix until thoroughly incorporated.

- Whip yogurt in a bowl, and add in a slow stream to the scalded milk while whisking vigorously to temper without curdling.
- Add yogurt mixture to the egg mixture and stir well. Once it is combined, add dry ingredients little by little and mix to form a batter. It should be thick like brownie batter.
- Grease a 9x13 baking dish and line it with 2 pieces of parchment paper to make a cradle with an overhang on all four sides. Grease the parchment paper too.
- Pour the prepared batter into the cake pan and bake in a preheated 375°F oven for 1 hour.
- Meanwhile, stir water, sugar, and cardamom powder in a saucepan. Cook until sugar dissolves. Once the sugar is dissolved and syrup is bubbly, stir in lemon juice and rose water. Remove from heat and let the syrup cool to room temperature.
- When the cake is ready, remove it from the oven and pour the syrup over the cake. It will look like it is too much syrup, but the cake will soak it all up.
- Scatter chopped pistachio all over the cake evenly. Lift the cake out of the pan with the parchment cradle onto a cutting board and cut into a 3x3 inch square. Cut the squares into triangles and place a pistachio in the center of each triangle,
- Arrange pieces on a platter to serve.

Puran Puris

½ pound all-purpose flour (use a scale, not cup measure)
Pinch salt
2 tablespoons butter
½ cup + 1 tablespoon whole milk to make a firm dough
Oil for frying
Filling:
2 sticks unsalted butter, or 1 cup pure ghee
1 inch cinnamon stick
1 cup Bengal gram dal
1½ cups sugar
¼ teaspoon cardamom powder
½ teaspoon saffron, crushed and soaked in 2 tablespoons milk
Or orange food color

- In a bowl, whisk flour and salt until blended, and then rub the butter in the flour until it resembles bread crumbs. Add milk to make the dough. Knead the dough until it is silky and smooth for about 10 minutes. Cover the dough with a wet cloth and set aside for 30 minutes. Knead again just before use. Meanwhile put Bengal gram dal in a saucepan with enough water to cover dal, and cook until very soft. Drain the water. Blend well with an immersion blender.
- Heat butter, or ghee in a saucepan, with a 1-inch cinnamon stick. When butter or ghee is melted and is very hot, add blended dal, sugar, saffron milk, or orange color, and cardamom powder and cook on moderately high heat. Continue to stir until all the moisture is dried out and the mixture is thick but not dry. Set aside to cool.
- Meanwhile, divide the dough into 10 small balls and roll each ball into a 6-inch round.
- Place one tablespoon of filling on the bottom half of each round, apply moisture to the edges and fold the top half over the filling making a half-

moon shape and seal well. Crimp the edges to make sure that the filling does not leak during frying.

- Heat enough oil for deep frying in a fryer or a frying pan. When the oil is hot, fry the puris in batches of two or three, depending on the size of the frying pan. Don't crowd the pan.
- When golden brown on one side, turn it over and let it brown on the other side also.
- Remove with a slotted spoon draining excess oil out of the puris.
- Serve just as, or with kheer for an added taste and texture.

Rasmalai

Rasmalai is an Indian treat that offers monumental bliss to your taste buds. I enjoy making this dessert tremendously. And I want everyone to try.

1 gallon whole milk
1-quart buttermilk
16-ounce Dragon whole milk Ricotta cheese
½ gallon half-and-half
3 ½ cups sugar, divided use
½ teaspoon finely powdered cardamom

- In a heavy saucepan bring milk to a slow boil.
- Also in another heavy saucepan, add half and half and bring to a simmer. When half-and-half is hot, add 16-ounce ricotta cheese, and 2 cups sugar and mix well to blend the ingredients into a smooth mixture. Lower heat to simmer and let it simmer until thick mixture.
- When the milk comes to a boil, add buttermilk and continue heating while stirring constantly until the milk solids separate from the water. As soon as the solids of milk curds (also called paneer) are separated, drain in a fine mesh colander and let it drip, and leave it until all the water is drained off. Let it cool completely. Transfer to a food processor.
- Meanwhile, in a heavy saucepan heat 6 to 8 cups water, add 1½ cup sugar and cardamom powder, and let it come to a boil. Let it simmer until all the sugar is dissolved and simple syrup is ready.
- Process the well-drained milk curds (paneer) in the food processor. Make 1 to 1½ inch balls, about 30, and put them in the syrup. Let them simmer for about 45 minutes. Remove from heat and let it cool to touch. Use your hands to remove the water out of the balls by pressing gently between the palms of your hands before dropping them into the prepared ricotta and half and half mixture.

- Try not to overload the mixture with too many balls to give room for each to swell after absorbing the ricotta mixture.
- Refrigerate for a few hours for the flavors to meld before serving.

Bibliography

Corriher O. Shirley: The Hows and Whys of Successful Baking with over200 magnificent recipes. New York: Scribner, 2008.

McGee, Harold. On Food and Cooking: The Science and love of the Kitchen. New York: Scribner, 1984.

Purdy, Susan. Have Your Cake and Eat It, Too. New York: William Morrow, 1993.

Mesnier, Roland, with Lauren Chattam. Dessert University. New York: Simon & Schuster, 2004.

Yard, Sherry. The Secrets of Baking: Simple Techniques for Sophisticated Desserts. Boston: Houghton Mifflin, 2003.

Paston-William, Sara. Country Cooking: Penguin Group. England. Print.

Greenspan, Dorie. Baking with Julia. New York: William Morrow and Company, 1996.

Walter, Carol. Great Pies & Tarts. New York: Clarkson Potter, 1998.

Braker, Flo. The Simple Art of Perfect Baking. Boston: Houghton Mifflin, 1997.

McGee, Harold. Keys to Good Cooking. New York: The Penguin Press, 2010.

Wolfert, Paula. The Cooking of South West France. Garden City, New York: The Dial Press/ Double day, 1983.

Ong, Pichet. Sweet Spot. New York: William Morrow Cookbooks, 2007.

Stewart, Martha, and Sarah Carey. Martha Stewart's Cooking School. New York: Clarkson Potter Publishers, 2008.

Strause, Monroe Boston. Pie Marches On, 2nd ed. New York: Aherns publishing Company, 1951.

Braker, Flo. Sweet Miniatures: The Art of Making Bite Size Desserts. Boston: Houghton Mifflin, 1991.

Norman, Jill, Editor in Chief. The Cook's Book: Techniques and tips

from the Worlds Master Chefs. England, 2005.
America's Test Kitchen, by the Editors. Cooking School Cookbook, 2013

index

O

P

Q

R

S

T

V

W

Printed in the USA
CPSIA information can be obtained
at www.ICGtesting.com
CBHW070108220824
13470CB00030B/674

9 781960 075161